Evaluating He

Evaluating Health and Social Care

Ceri Phillips

Colin Palfrey

and

Paul Thomas

MACMILLAN

First published 1994 by
THE MACMILLAN PRESS LTD
Houndmills, Basingstoke, Hampshire RG21 2XS
and London
Companies and representatives
throughout the world

ISBN 0-333-59185-2 hardcover
ISBN 0-333-59186-0 paperback

A catalogue record for this book is available from the British Library.

Copy-edited and typeset by Povey-Edmondson
Okehampton and Rochdale, England

Printed in Hong Kong

Contents

List of Figures and Tables

Figures

Tables

Preface

The origins of this book may be traced to the submission of a tender for a research contract to evaluate two major innovative programmes in the field of health and social care. Each of the authors had been interested in the notion of evaluation in the field of health and social care from the perspective of his respective discipline. There was thus a common factor –the field of health and social care – but also many conflicting and opposing views, grounded in the wide variety of approaches and frameworks available to potential evaluators.

We came to the conclusion that there is no one *best* approach to adopt; each has its merits and limitations. Our own preference is for a framework which combines a number of approaches in such a way that the methods chosen for evaluation are appropriate to the situation and context of the policy being examined. This approach, we argue, removes some of the biases of the discipline based approach and provides a rich and realistic picture in which both successes and failures can be identified. It is not, however, a panacea for problems of evaluation and it is certainly not *neutral* in any absolute sense. However, we believe that it is likely to be the most useful approach for evaluating policies and programmes in the field of health and social care.

Agencies within health and social care are under increasing pressure to evaluate and improve their performance, for example to measure effectiveness and efficiency and to assess the degree of satisfaction amongst the consumers of their services. The book aims to provide a practical guide for managers, professionals and students who wish to evaluate the performance of social care and health agencies.

Chapter 1 endeavours to answer the question 'What is Evaluation?', whilst at the same time demonstrating the limitations of less comprehensive approaches to monitoring and evaluation and emphasising the need to involve the users of services at all stages of the evaluation process.

Chapter 2 deals with evaluation designs and methods, reviewing a range of designs that may be used in constructing an evaluation and considering the types of data that may need to be collected and how they can be collected. It also describes how the data can be checked for its validity and reliability and offers an introduction to the ways in which data can be analysed so as to generate appropriate findings for an evaluation.

Chapters 3–7 explore the main criteria available for evaluating health and social care: effectiveness, efficiency, organisational structures and processes, equality, equity, accessibility and how consumer opinions can be used in the evaluation process. Each chapter explains why these criteria are used, identifies the problems inherent in using them and offers specific guidance on how to use each of the criteria.

CERI PHILLIPS
COLIN PALFREY
PAUL THOMAS

1

What is Evaluation?

Evaluation

'Evaluation' is concerned with judging merit against some yardstick. It involves the collection, analysis and interpretation of data bearing on the achievement of an organisation's goals and programme objectives. Evaluation usually attempts to measure the extent to which certain *outcomes* can be validly correlated with *inputs* and/or *outputs*. The aim is to establish whether there is a cause–effect relationship.

Not all evaluation, however, is concerned with outcomes (defined rather narrowly at this stage as 'the impact of services upon intended beneficiaries'). For some years, particularly in the health care sector, attention has been paid to service *inputs*, *throughputs* and *outputs*. These are quantifiable indicators of performance and provide evidence of the extent to which specified targets are being met. The stipulation of the Patients' Charter (1992) that no one should wait more than two years for any treatment provided by the National Health Service is an example of a *throughput* of patients.

Within the social care context, a local authority could decide as part of its Social Care Plan to respond to a call for assistance within a specified number of hours or days to make sure that an initial visit is made to a prospective service user within one week. These highly specific targets are known as *performance* or *key indicators*.

How does evaluation differ from monitoring?

Monitoring, involving the systematic and continuous surveillance of a series of events, is more concerned with *procedures* and *processes*. Trying to evaluate how well we are doing in providing services will, of course, mean that in many cases it will be essential to monitor what is going on, although it is conceivable that evaluation could be carried out without this continuing surveillance. For example, a new system of staff appraisal could be introduced and after six months a sample of staff could be asked as part of an evaluation what they thought of the new system in terms of its effect upon staff morale and motivation.

In many cases, a combination of monitoring and evaluation will provide a much fuller and more sensitive analysis of a developing situation. Where there is continuous feedback during the course of a programme or project, this is called *formative evaluation*. The evaluation carried out after the programme or project has finished is called *summative evaluation*. Formative evaluation involves stage by stage comparison between stated objectives of a programme and what is actually being achieved. A brief example will help to distinguish between monitoring, formative evaluation and summative evaluation.

Example: the Quality Action Group

Senior management staff in a social services department decided that they wished to involve users of a day centre and residential centre in decisions which affected their experience of care. Both day care and residential facilities occupied the same site in a purpose-built modern complex. It was, therefore, decided to arrange a meeting in order to explain the purpose of what was to be called a Quality Action Group (QAG) made up of representatives of senior management, centre staff, users, carers and voluntary helpers. The decision was also made to commission an observer from outside the authority's area to record, monitor and evaluate what might be called a 'journey towards user empowerment'.

After preliminary discussions amongst all participants an agenda was drafted for the first meeting. During the course of this meeting there emerged a number of issues which users felt ought to be defined as target objectives for the purpose of evaluating the 'success' of this new approach to service planning and provision after an agreed period of time. There was also a need to provide continuous feedback to members of the QAG on how the observer perceived progress towards enhanced user empowerment.

Strategic goals

Strategic goals such as 'empowerment' are rarely defined. Therefore, they have to be operationally defined in terms of explicitly stated *objectives*. In this case, a number of key questions were identified to form the basis of the monitoring and evaluation; those set out below are merely a few examples.

Process
- Who set the agenda?
- Who chaired the meetings?
- Was the chairperson elected or selected?
- To what extent did users appear to be confident in expressing their views?

Output
- What formal response to the minutes of the meetings was received by the QAG from senior management and the social services committee?
- What changes were implemented as a result of the QAG's recommendations?
- How long did it take for any changes to be brought into effect?
- At what level of decision-making (i.e. day to day, strategic, budgetary) did the QAG operate?

Outcomes
- What benefits, if any, did the various members of the QAG consider to have been brought about as a result of their meetings?

- On a personal level, did users feel that they now had greater control over their lives within the day care and residential settings?
- In what aspects, if any, of their daily living did users and carers feel more 'empowered'?

Charting the journey

The *monitoring element* – as far as the observer was concerned – involved logging events as they happened. The *formative evaluation* drew upon the contents of the log in order to act as the compass, relaying observed events and behaviour back to the members, seeing if they agreed with this, and deciding collectively whether the programme was still on course or whether on occasions it was drifting away. At the end of the period set aside for the programme of meetings, the *summative evaluation* attempted to answer the question:

'Have we arrived at our destination?'
If 'no', where are we?
If 'yes' or 'no', how did we arrive there?
If 'yes' or 'no', is it worth going on?

Why bother to evaluate services?

In a service industry such as tourism or catering the profit motive supplies reason enough for building into an organisation's thinking and operations an element of marketing research. This is especially relevant when there is strong evidence to indicate that the most financially successful companies – whether service, manufacturing or other – have a track record of knowing their customers and responding to their expressed needs or wishes.

In the public sector, such as the health services and local authority social services, profit is not usually the incentive for attempting to match products or services to consumers' requirements. It is not within the remit of this book to suggest reasons why service evaluation and a consumer-led approach to planning and provision have become so prominent in political and professional policy statements. Suffice to say that just as poverty was 're-discovered' in the relatively affluent 1950s, so the public service consumer has been identified in the 1980s and 1990s as a person with rights over and above mere statutory entitlements.

In this new scenario of consumerism and a mixed economy of care the intended beneficiary of health and care services is moving slowly towards centre stage. In attempting to match resources and services to clients' or patients' expectations and perceived needs, health and social services staff at all levels are entering an entirely new arena. The concern to provide the best possible care and support has always been the main concern of health and social work practitioners. Until recently, however, the over-riding aim has been to improve efficiency. Now the quest for effectiveness has entered the list. As one writer on management neatly put it, we have added to the question: 'Are we doing things right?' the equally, if not more important question: 'Are we doing the right things?' (Drucker, 1968).

Quality assurance and quality control

Quality assurance and quality control

Evaluation of services – as subsequent chapters in this book will make clear – may need to refer to a number of criteria in order to measure merit against certain yardsticks. Two of these criteria are efficiency and effectiveness. In recent years, the NHS – more so than social services authorities – has paid particular attention to issues related to quality. In fact, the word 'quality' has come to pervade literature and reports about health service management and health service delivery. 'Quality adjusted life-years' (QALYs) has become a very potent conceptual tool for attempting to gauge the effect of health care interventions on the patient's future quantity and quality of life. 'Quality circles' (QCs) have been set up in health authorities as a response to the commitment to 'Total Quality Management' (TQM).

Central to all these relatively new ideas is the concept of 'Quality Assurance' (QA) and central to quality assurance is the need for evaluation. *Quality Assurance* demands a commitment to the pursuit of a high standard of services. This demand – as we have indicated in the preceding paragraph – is not new. What is new is the articulation in public policy documents of how the authorities expect to see quality of service made manifest. Policy statements setting out performance indicators and stressing the essential role of monitoring and evaluation of services appear in strategic planning documents of both health and social work authorities.

Quality Control (QC) refers to the means by which articulated standards and service objectives will be measured against actual performance.

Mechanisms of quality control

To some extent, the term 'quality control' would seem to be a somewhat inappropriate concept. The word 'control' carries the connotation of modulating rather than enhancing standards of service – as if quality should not exceed predetermined levels. This is not a semantic quibble. Until very recently, a reasonable analogy with the world of manufacturing industry could well have been applied to the realms of health and social services. Just as the product in the factory needed to conform as closely as possible to its original design and functioning specifications, so the various service products of health and social care agencies were assessed according to similar criteria.

The range of services – for example, acute care, chronic care, day centres, residential establishments, domiciliary care, outpatient services – were all designed by professionals and administrators for use by patients or clients. Judgements as to whether these services were up to standard were based much more on criteria such as staffing levels, patient throughputs, waiting times for operations, numbers of meals on wheels delivered, staff-patient/client ratios, morbidity and mortality rates than on the quality of the caring process itself or the effect of interventions as perceived by patients/clients. So the traditional mechanisms for assessing standards in health and social care have sought answers to the question: 'Are we doing things right?' rather than 'Are we doing the right things?' We list below some of these mechanistic approaches to controlling quality of care.

1. *Inspection*

The idea that inspection within the public sector can yield only a snapshot of an organisation's activities and performance may be less than fair. Within the field of education, for example, inspection can range from a fairly cursory review of curricula, teaching practices and resources to a full-scale in-depth analysis of the whole institutional 'fabric' and its relationship with the external environment and with current national policy and expected performance.

Until recently, 'inspection' as a function of social services departments came to be equated with committee members' rota visits to residential homes. These occasions did, indeed, produce somewhat perfunctory and limited reviews of mainly physical standards within the homes. Since the NHS and Community Care Act of 1990 inspection units have had to be set up in social services departments at 'arm's length' from the management function. Initially these units will carry out inspections of homes within the independent sector, but there is also a responsibility to monitor standards in the department's own residential establishments.

Inspection has a role to play in quality control in the sense of maintaining prescribed standards of care. Nor will its role be confined as in the past to concentrating on the physical amenities and environment. Inspection will need to take into account the way in which the home is managed, including the range of opportunities residents have to exercise choice. The snapshot will develop as much more of a three-dimensional picture.

In the NHS the first moves towards at least a quasi-inspectorate followed the revelations of the standards of patient care at Ely Hospital in Cardiff. As a result of the enquiry a Hospital Advisory Service was created in 1960 and this changed its name in 1976 to the Health Advisory Service. Its remit now includes not only hospitals but community services and long-stay facilities for children. Visits to the range of health authority facilities are made by medical practitioners, managers and social services colleagues but there may be gaps of ten years between such visits.

As a device to appraise the quality of care inspection has its shortcomings:

Limitations of inspection

- Because a relatively small number of staff have to cover all the facilities within their remit visits to each establishment are infrequent. Inspection cannot, therefore, closely monitor the process of care or engage in an in-depth analysis of interactions between staff and users or between staff and colleagues.
- Those who carry out the inspection in social services departments may have to visit establishments owned and run by the very authority of which they are members or paid employees. The issue of how objective these assessments may be is a potential problem.
- Inspectors, whether from a central inspectorate such as the Department of Health or the Welsh Office or from a social services department, look at the situation from their own perspective. There is little opportunity to involve users and carers in the inspection exercise.

2. *Reviews*

The idea of a review is that an organisation should prepare its plans on a regular basis and that progress towards the achievement of objectives and targets set out in those plans should be subjected to scrutiny. Since their inception in 1974 the amalgamated social services departments have been obliged to produce plans which formed the authority's blueprint for service development over five and sometimes ten years. These proposals are then sent to the appropriate government department (DHSS, now the Department of Health and the Welsh or Scottish Office) for approval. With the passage of the NHS and Community Care Act in 1990 departments have to prepare Social Care Plans in accordance with guidelines laid down by central government. The plans have to be approved by the appropriate government department before they can be used as strategic and operational planning documents.

Within the NHS a review procedure was not instituted until 1982 when ministerial reviews of Regional Health Authorities (RHAs) were set in train. These reviews concentrated on the longer-term strategic component of policy statements. In order to ensure that the shorter term operational elements of plans were also monitored, the RHAs reviewed District Health Authority (DHA) plans and DHAs in turn reviewed the work at unit level.

Limitations of reviews

- The main concern of reviews is the extent to which service organisations conform to their approved plans. Issues of efficiency and budgeting take precedence over questions of the appropriateness, responsiveness and effectiveness of services.
- Although patient or client representatives may be consulted during the process of devising the plans they are primarily the domain of senior management staff. The views and expectations of field level practitioners or users and informal carers may be canvassed but are not paramount other than in such avowed mission statements as 'putting patients first' or 'empowering users'.

- It is questionable whether reviews exert any measurable impact upon the quality of public care services. The inevitably 'broad brush' approach emphasises lines of accountability upwards at the expense of helping to reinforce practical ways in which a commitment to user-led services might be improved.

3. *Medical audit*

A report published in 1987 into peri-operative deaths focused attention on the effectiveness and quality of in-patient surgery. Some senior surgeons and anaesthetists had been concerned about the considerable variance in peri-operative mortality rates for the same condition treated in different hospitals or by different surgeons. As a result, consultants in health authorities were asked to participate in a confidential enquiry.

This forum for peer review was greeted enthusiastically by the government who decided to set up a medical audit committee in each health district. The extent to which this form of quality control will be able to influence practice remains to be proved. In this sphere of peer review, as with inspection and review by ministers or civil servants, implementing changes as a consequence of inadequate or incompetent performance is problematic. Confidentiality, professional ethics and organisational resistance to change may conspire to impede specific remedial action.

Another professional initiative towards monitoring professional standards was the system of practice assessment established in the mid-1970s by the Royal College of General Practitioners (RCGP). RCGP assessors visited GP practices and attempted to rate them under three headings: clinical competence, accessibility and ability to communicate. The White Paper *Working for Patients* (Department of Health, 1989) adopted this more user-focused approach to assessing the quality of the caring process rather than relying on statistical indices of outputs and outcomes as proxy measures of effectiveness (Harrison *et al.*, 1990). Medical audit as a means of improving the efficiency and quality of health and welfare of patients has been criticised (Hopkins, 1991; Maynard, 1991). Some of these criticisms are summarised below.

Limitations of medical audit

- Because they are reviews by members of the same profession their findings are confidential. There is, therefore, no opportunity for lay people – whether individually or in representative groups – to bring pressure to bear on the government, health authorities, Family Health Service Authorities or GP practices with a view to improving upon identified weak areas.
- Intended beneficiaries of the services or competencies under review take no part in drawing up the criteria against which performance is to be gauged.
- Peer review, therefore, has no contribution to make toward clarifying which aspects of clinician – patient relationships should receive priority attention in future strategic and operational planning.
- Even if medical audits are able to improve clinical practice there is no guarantee that improvements will occur in areas relevant to raising levels of patient satisfaction.

4. *Performance indicators (PIs)*

Since the 1980s both health and social care organisations have received a form of guidance from central government which has used comparative data in order to compare particular aspects of 'performance'. Social services departments' annual returns to the government have provided the basis for producing yardsticks. These have been construed almost as targets for the departments to attain since they appear to reflect the national picture. For example, from annual returns the number of home care organisers per 10,000 population aged 75 and over can be computed on a nationwide basis.

Statistics of this kind cannot form the basis of national or county policy decision-making without further analysis. Only then can their interpretation begin to extract meaning from mere figures. For example, consider the following very simple set of statistics:

County X employs 1 fieldworker per 5,000 population
County Y employs 3 fieldworkers per 5,000 population

Without further investigation any of these inferences may be drawn:

1 County X is understaffed
2 County Y is overstaffed
3 County X is more efficient than County Y
4 County Y has proportionately more people in need of social work intervention than County X

Other inferences are capable of being drawn, and their validity can only be established by digging deeper. Perhaps County Y is more rural in topography than County X and, therefore, has set up a system of decentralised offices to counteract travelling time. Referral procedures may be different and we do not know, for example, whether 'need' is interpreted differently in one county compared with the other. Clearly, unless knowledge of the geographical, demographical and socio-economic profile of the administrative areas is made available the bald statistics make very little sense. This knowledge, too, will need to be supplemented by information about the way in which services are organised in each county, and about the nature and policy of the organisation itself.

Performance indicators become more significant in terms of monitoring aspects of service planning and operation when they appear in social services departments' policy statements.

These are usually set out as targets which are easily measured provided that recording practices are meticulous. Here are some examples.

- All telephone enquiries from members of the public will be referred to an appropriate member of staff within three minutes of the call being received.
- All written enquiries from members of the public will be replied to within three working days.
- All Part III Homes will be closed and all former residents placed in community settings within two years from (a specified) date.
- The number of children between the ages of 10 and 17 referred to the courts for criminal offences will be reduced by 50% over the next five years.

The application of PIs in the NHS has been more formalised than in the field of social work practice. In the early 1980s the DHSS devised nearly 150 PIs to cover performance in the areas of clinical practice, finance, staffing, support services and other aspects of adminstration. The intention was for all Regional and District Health Authorities to gather a nation-wide picture of performance against which their own performance could be gauged. Some particular indicators are:

- the average number of patients per bed per year
- the average waiting time for certain operations
- the average length of stay in hospital per medical speciality
- the number of in-patient admissions per 10,000 population (Harrison *et al.*, 1990).

The compilation of a set of statistical data which can provide an accurate, if superficial, account of what is happening throughout the country depends on each authority's capacity to provide its own accurate and comprehensive data. Performance indicators founder on inadequate information and recording systems and unless these are subjected to continuous external and internal scrutiny there is no guarantee that the composite national statistics bear much comparison with reality.

Limitations of performance indicators

- Although their ultimate aim may be to improve standards of care, the preparation of PIs does not involve the intended beneficiaries of care.
- Their quantitative nature stresses procedures, throughputs and outputs rather than outcomes and effectiveness.
- Their superficiality debars them from having much validity in terms of initiating policy at either local or national level.
- Their compilation presupposes that each contributing authority has accurate and comprehensive and comparable information systems.
- They take no account of variations in the priority given by different authorities to aspects of their care services.

5. *Satisfaction surveys*

Asking people what they think of current health and social care services adds another dimension to the more mechanistic approaches described above. The results of patient satisfaction surveys feature prominently in health and particularly nursing literature. Many social services departments also canvass opinions from users, carers, voluntary organisations and the public generally about the appropriateness and accessibility of services. On a national scale, professional market research agencies have administered opinion polls to a sample of the population about their views on the NHS.

Chapter 6 will deal more fully with the whole approach to seeking people's opinions about services. The collection of qualitative, highly personal data offers another perspective on the issue of service planning and provision. But satisfaction surveys alone will not counterbalance the 'top down' attempts to assess performance. The statutory complaints procedures which social services authorities now have to operate afford an opportunity for aggrieved members of the public to have their say. The issue here – as with all efforts at compiling information about 'how we are doing' – is the 'So what?' question. In other words, what action is taken to improve matters as a result of the information gathered?

The danger with carrying out user or public surveys is that the very act of conducting a piece of consumer or market research may come to be treated as an end rather than a means. Another potential shortcoming is the almost universal recourse to a questionnaire as the method of data collection. Even the most experienced, professional constructors of questionnaires are likely to produce relatively flawed products. The assumption that almost anyone with sufficient motivation can compose a reliable and valid questionnaire is very unwise. The need to approach qualitative data collection using a combination of research instruments is emphasised in Chapter 6.

The limitations outlined below do not undermine the potential usefulness of opinion surveys. As with all efforts to reflect upon professional and organisational performance they have a part to play.

Limitations of satisfaction surveys

- They often assume that the person asked has a knowledge of alternative treatment or caring practices.
- Satisfaction with a service does not tell us much about the actual quality of that service since the respondent may be starting from a very low level of expectation about standards.

- Unless we are able to correlate degrees of satisfaction with the individual's previous experience of similar services any comparative data about services in other places or at other points in that person's life can not be assessed.
- Data is often derived from questionnaires when alternative or additional research methods, such as individual or group interviews, case studies and personal diaries might yield richer and more valid data.

Formal evaluation

Formal evaluation, which is a method of enquiry founded upon the principles of social research rather than a form of evaluation derived entirely from personal experience, custom and practice or a 'gut feeling', has many advantages over the approaches described above. First of all it moves a distance from the more mechanistic *quality control* to what may be termed *quality appraisal*. We have noted that quality control mechanisms operate from a top-down perspective. Certain expected standards of performance – usually quantifiable – are laid down by senior management, professional practitioners or by the government and an exercise is periodically conducted to compare expectation with achievement.

Evaluation (in the sense of formal evaluation) is more open-ended. It uses criteria which have to do with the impact of care upon individuals and/or groups of people while it may also be concerned with issues of cost–benefit and efficiency. In other words, it has the capacity – depending on the purpose of the programme or practices to be evaluated – to take a much broader view of what is understood by the term 'quality'.

What is 'quality'?

Not every product that is bought by consumers is manufactured with quality in mind. Durability of materials is probably one of the hallmarks of a quality product but for the consumer convenience and cheapness may be more attractive attributes. 'Disposability' rather than 'durability' may prove to be the selling point: the purchase of disposable razors, pens and even cameras testifies to this area of consumer preference. The decision to buy one product rather than any other may in a way be simplified by a person's very limited means. The crucial concern here is probably the issue of *value for money*. This is not, however, some objectively definable concept. It involves a strong element of 'taste'. In the literal sense someone may prefer eating beefburgers and chips to French haute cuisine even though they could well afford either and even though they would accept that in terms of a quality product the French meal is superior. In this example, the satisfaction or pleasure derived from an 'inferior' product is the primary concern.

In other areas of consumer choice, people's personal experience of satisfaction or pleasure gained by use of a particular product can over-ride an awareness that its use may, in fact, be harmful. Smoking and the abuse of controlled drugs provide obvious examples. Quality, therefore, is a highly personalised concept and the important message for health and care services is to begin to ask questions about *whose quality* ought to be controlled or appraised.

Quality of life and quality of care

Relevant to this question is the distinction that needs to be made between *quality of life* and *quality of care*. In terms of evaluation, we can say that the more dominant concern of health and social care has been quality of care and that the developing policy of user-led service provision now has to address issues relating to quality of life. Since judgements about quality of life can best be made by, rather than on behalf of, individual human beings, the need to involve users and potential users in planning care packages and treatment and care programmes becomes paramount. Exceptions may need to be made in the case of people who have profound learning difficulties or others who are unable to communicate their perceived needs and preferences. In these instances, advocates – be they family, friends, voluntary or statutory helpers – may need to be involved.

It is quite easy to conceive of a situation symptomatic of traditional modes of service planning and delivery in which an excellent quality of care is provided which adds nothing or véry little to a person's quality of life. This happens when there is a lack of compatibility between producer and consumer expectations about the most desirable service.

Example: Mrs Green

Mrs Green is an 80-year-old widow who lives on her own in a bungalow. She is no longer very mobile because of severe arthritis. She has few contacts outside her home.

The health and social service authorities are aware of Mrs Green's physical and social limitations and have consulted each other about a joint care package. The district nurse visits Mrs Green once a week to check whether she is taking the correct dosages of tablets prescribed to ease her pain. The occupational therapist also visits Mrs Green once a week to help her carry out basic exercises to maintain a degree of mobility and the social services department has arranged to transport her twice a week to a day centre for lunch and social activities.

Mrs Green is very grateful for all these services and has no complaints about the manner in which staff attend to her 'needs'. Why then is she still not contented? Actually, if Mrs Green had to choose just one form of help she would opt for someone to do her front garden once a week. When her husband was alive and when, after being widowed, she was much fitter, the garden was her pride and joy. If only it wasn't looking so overgrown and it could be restored to its former neatness and colour and maintained that way she would put up with not going out and lack of mobility. Her satisfaction and great pleasure would be derived from sitting in her front window admiring her garden and watching the world go by.

The mismatch here between quality of care and quality of life has to do with different interpretations of priority 'need' and of 'appropriateness'.

Criteria for evaluating high quality performance

Maxwell (1984) has devised a set of criteria which can help to indicate the standard of performance in a health care agency. The criteria can be summarised as follows:

1	**effectiveness**	–	the extent to which objectives are achieved
2	**efficiency**	–	the ratio of benefits to costs
3	**equity**	–	equal treatment for equal needs
4	**appropriateness**	–	relevance to need
5	**acceptability**	–	to individuals, groups and society at large
6	**accessibility**	–	in terms, e.g. of time and location.

These criteria, which will be examined throughout this book, are an interesting list of considerations which a providing or commissioning agency may well use in order to evaluate the quality of care, but not all may be relevant to assessing the extent to which quality of life is enhanced.

Users of health and social care services are unlikely to be interested in broad questions of efficiency or equity, and what if producer and consumer opinions differ about what constitutes effectiveness, appropriateness, acceptability and accessibility? If, in attempting to evaluate services, we were to look through the consumer's eyes and ask 'What is quality?' the answer might be relatively straightforward. A quality service is 'one that gives me what I want'.

Clarification of key terms

At the beginning of this chapter, evaluation was described as a task in which merit was judged against some yardstick and it was stated that evaluation was concerned with quality assurance. Further discussion has moved to a position where we have associated monitoring as an attempt to answer the question: 'Are we doing things right?' and evaluation as a formal exercise in appraising quality. We have also noted that attempts to evaluate the quality of care have more to do with process, and that evaluating the effect of that process upon its recipients is concerned with measuring quality of life as an outcome. At this point it is as well that key terms are clarified:

1 **procedure** – accordance with formalised rules and regulations
2 **process** – a series of actions and interactions
3 **inputs** – resources invested in specified official activities
4 **outputs** – a measurable product attributable to an input or combination of inputs
5 **outcome** – an end-state which may or may not be the intended effect of specified inputs, outputs or processes.

Example: the mentally ill in the community

An experimental community care project initiated by a health authority aims to maintain elderly mentally ill people in their own homes and prevent for as long as possible their admission to long-stay wards in a hospital.

- *Inputs* include the appointment to the scheme of specially trained home support workers, earmarked funding from central government and the health authority and management and administrative costs.

- The *process* of setting up the project, informing potential users, relatives and staff in the health authority, social services department and voluntary agencies is considered crucial to the twin objectives of interprofessional collaboration and to the need to let the intended beneficiaries know what the project is setting out to do.
- *Outputs* have been designated for each client. These include home support, pendants connected to a night alarm system and organised visits to a day centre.
- The anticipated *outcomes* are an enhanced satisfaction experienced by users and informal carers compared with the situation prior to the project's launch and the maintenance of elderly people in their own homes who, without the scheme's existence, would be patients in hospital.

After an agreed period in which the project has been in operation data is analysed. This shows that the elderly people on the scheme and/or their advocates are happy with the way in which care is given and admission to hospital on a long-stay basis has been considerably delayed. Careful evaluation will enable us to know whether these findings are a coincidence or whether they can be directly linked to a component or set of components exclusive to the experimental programme. As Chapter 2 will indicate, answers to this central question hinge on issues concerning research design and methodology.

Who should carry out evaluation?

The sheer complexity involved in much evaluation demands a degree of initiation into the ground rules of social research principles, designs and methods. Chapter 2 deals with these matters in some detail. In particular, those evaluation studies which seek to examine whether certain inputs and/or outputs are the cause of identifiable outcomes pose problems of methodology, analysis and, in some instances, of ethics. This suggests that appropriately trained academics rather than lay-people are better able to carry out formal evaluation. This may be true in the more sophisticated research designs but this need not be a general rule.

What if staff and users or their advocates become involved in the evaluation research? Will this not compromise the objectivity needed to conduct research? There are a number of issues here. First of all, lay-people can be 'involved with' evaluation without actually taking on the role of researcher. There are strong grounds for arguing that users and potential users should be in at the very early stages of evaluation (for example, Martin, 1986). They ought to be involved at the research proposal and research design stages, and should be consulted about the purpose of the evaluation and about the criteria to be applied as yardsticks for measurement. If the evaluation exercise is intended to be an integral part of quality assurance then those for whom services are to be designed need to have a major say in what, for example, could legitimately be regarded as 'effective'. Users and potential users of services can be, and indeed ought to be, involved.

Discussions about the most appropriate methods of *data collection* may need to be led by someone well acquainted with the range of methods, with their strengths and weaknesses and with their application. Apart from contributing to the research by answering questions, keeping diaries and being observed there are good reasons for offering users an opportunity for more active participation in the evaluation. Once a questionnaire or interview schedule has been devised there is no particular mystique involved in making sure that questions are answered as honestly as possible. Indeed, the presence of a user rather than a researcher might prompt a higher degree of honesty.

Observation – as Chapter 2 points out – can be a very rewarding method of 'getting at' suppressed information and gaining insights into a range of social behaviour. The crucial points at which behaviour is being observed and interpreted calls for checks against bias and filtering of signals. The deployment of users and staff as observers can supply these checks. Attempts to achieve a high degree of objectivity in carrying out research are intended to prevent personal opinion, whim, hunch, tub-thumping or prejudice from becoming the dominant factor in collecting and analysing data. Academics bring their own form of subjectivity to each research project.

We propose, therefore, that a collaborative approach to formal evaluation be adopted involving representatives of all interested parties at all stages of the evaluation process except, perhaps, for the computer analysis of data if that is required. Much has been written above about the more mechanistic methods of monitoring performance. Collaborative evaluation offers a much less 'top-down' approach. Research findings and any resulting plans for action are much more likely to be accepted by users when they have been involved in the whole evaluation enterprise.

Honesty as a management virtue

There is no surer way of raising users' expectations than to involve them in the evaluation of services. Even the rudimentary level of involvement such as responding to questions put by an outside researcher stimulates a prospect of change. It is, therefore, absolutely vital that the health care agency, social services department or independent organisation commissioning or carrying out the evaluation should think through the possible implications of the research findings. By this we do not mean that the results will be anticipated or known before the evaluation is even started. What we are saying is that those who have power over resources should be honest about the magnitude of change which is feasible and, indeed, whether they are committed to acting upon – if any action is needed – the messages transmitted by the evaluation research findings.

Although a number of health and social services authorities embark upon the evaluation of major programmes which may run for three or more years, a general rule should be: 'Think big; act small' (Bryson, 1988). This suggests that organisations should always plan strategically on a grand scale by developing long-term policies but be prepared to move incrementally towards ultimate goals. Not all evaluation research, for example, should seek to establish principles of service design which can be transferable across other authorities, other regions or even nationally. The more modest, highly contextual evidence generated by smaller-scale but no less innovative approaches to improving people's quality of life may be extremely, if only locally, significant.

For example, a pilot scheme to place all trainees in one adult training centre in work situations in the local community might produce evaluation research data which is potentially applicable nationwide. On the other hand, the findings – assuming that they were to show a high incidence of 'genuine' work placements as a result of the initiative – could be attributable to local conditions, e.g. a very large manufacturer located in the area might have decided to adopt a policy of taking on former trainees.

Evaluation as a revolutionary activity

Another reason for thinking big and acting small is that evaluation and its concern with a consumer orientated approach to services has no history in the fields of health and social care. No one, therefore, should try to run before they can walk. The concept of user empowerment, in the name of which many new schemes are being set up and evaluated, is breathtakingly radical in its implications for shifts of power and influence in service planning and modes of service provision. Small-scale but nonetheless rigorous developments and innovations can, during the course of their evaluation enable staff, volunteers, users and advocates to become confident in the use of evaluation principles and techniques. The rest of this book is designed to assist in this process.

Summary and checklist

The various elements of formal evaluation have been set out in this chapter. The adoption of a 'systems model' as a framework for carrying out evaluation has been proposed, i.e. the links between inputs, outputs and outcomes have been identified as well as the process by which tasks and objectives are pursued. Discussion of these issues has been placed within the framework of organisational and national concerns for quality assurance and official recognition through the medium of White Papers, legislation and health and social services planning statements of the obligation to place users of services at the heart of care planning and evaluation:

The following checklist focuses attention on those questions relating to the planning of a formal evaluation:

1 Are all parties to the evaluation agreed on the criteria to be used as yardsticks?
2 For what purposes will the results of the evaluation be used?
3 Is there a commitment by the commissioning agency to act upon any proposals for change which the evaluation findings may be indicating?
4 Is any such commitment realistic in terms of any potential increase in resources that implementing change may require?
5 Who will carry out the evaluation, and for what reasons?
6 Will the evaluation be formative, summative or a combination of the two?

References

Bryson, J. (1988) 'Strategic planning: big wins and small wins', *Public Money and Management* (Autumn), pp. 11–15.

Connolly, N. and Goldberg, E. M. (eds) (1980) *Evaluative Research in Social Care*, Heinemann, London.

Department of Health (1989) *Working for Patients*, Cmnd. 555, London: HMSO.

Drucker, P. (1968) *The Practice of Management*, Heinemann, London.

Harrison, S., Hunter, D. J. and Pollitt, C. (1990) *The Dynamics of British Health Policy*, Unwin Hyman, London.
Holland, W. W. (ed.) (1983) *Evaluation of Health Care*, Oxford University Press.
Hopkins, A. (1991) 'Approaches to medical audit', *Journal of Epidemiology and Community Health*, 45, pp. 1–3.
Jowett, P. (1989) *Performance Indicators in the Public Sector*, Macmillan, London.
Martin, E. (1986) 'Consumer evaluation of human services', *Social Policy and Administration*, 20(3), pp. 185–200.
Maynard, A. (1991) 'Case for auditing audit', *Health Service Journal* (18 July), p. 26.
Maxwell, R. J. (1984) 'Quality assessment in health care', *British Medical Journal*, 288, pp. 166–203.
Pollitt, C. (1986) 'Measuring performance: a new system for the NHS', *Policy and Politics,* 13 (1), pp. 1–15.
Rossi, P. H. and Freeman, H. (1985) *Evaluation: a systematic approach*, Sage, Beverly Hills.
Smith, G. and Cantley, C. (1985) *Assessing Health Care: a study in organisational evaluation*, Open University Press, Milton Keynes.
St Leger, A. S. *et al.* (1992) *Evaluating Health Services' Effectiveness*, Open University Press, Milton Keynes.

2

Evaluation Research Designs and Methods

The planning of any evaluation requires careful thought about the type of investigation to be carried out, the variety of data required, how this will be collected and checked in terms of its reliability and validity and the sort of analysis necessary to produce appropriate findings. This chapter provides some insights into these areas, beginning with the design stage of an evaluation and moving on to the range of methods that can be used in undertaking evaluations in the field of health and social care.

Designing an evaluation

In order to produce data which is both reliable and valid the evaluation needs to be systematic and structured. The term *formal evaluation* sums up this approach. The *design* of a programme of formal evaluation indicates this systematic approach by specifying a research plan which is appropriate to the purpose of the evaluation.

Most attempts at evaluating aspects of health and social care set out to discover the efficiency and/or effectiveness of service provision. They are, therefore, more than descriptive because they seek to test the impact of processes and outputs on service users or on specific aspects of the providing organisation. This requires programme objectives to be stated clearly and in a form which is amenable to some method of assessment or measurement. The purpose of most formal evaluation is to produce evidence which will enable those evaluating to determine the extent to which a factor (or factors) affects the course of events.

The problem lies in identifying exactly which factors have exerted any influence – those purposely built into a particular programme or those which may have just 'happened'. The technical term for these factors is *variables*, and the problem of identifying influencing factors is referred to as the problem of *controlling the variables.*

Types of evaluation designs

All formal evaluation involves an element of comparison:

- we might wish to compare a person's health before and after an operation
- we might want to compare one kind of medical treatment with another on persons with similar illnesses
- the benefits of social services may be compared over time or with each other
- the uptake of social security benefits among a sample group could be measured before and after an intensive publicity drive
- the capacity for ex-hospital patients to cope in the community could be assessed by focusing on two comparable sets of former patients, one of which gets daily support from social workers and another which is not given any external support.

Comparisons may be made at different points in time and/or between comparable groups exposed to different variables – one of which might be a 'placebo' or non-intervention. We now turn to some examples of these comparative evaluation designs: it should be emphasised that they are not mutually exclusive.

Experimental

This classic scientific design is best illustrated by the clinical trials carried out by members of the medical profession. In experimental designs two groups receive differing interventions – an experimental group and a control group. The latter group consists of persons who are as similar as possible in key attributes to those in the experimental group. This is done in order to control as many variables as possible which, in turn, will allow valid inferences to be drawn about the impact of some intervention on members of the experimental group (E group). To construct a truly equivalent control group it is important to assign individuals randomly to each group so that factors influencing outcomes will be evenly distributed to each programme from the outset.

There are variations on the experimental design. For instance, in order to enhance objectivity a *'blind' experiment* could be carried out, where the researcher does not know who is in the experimental group, and hence receiving 'treatment', and who is in the control group, and hence receiving the 'placebo'.

This can be further developed by the use of a *'double-blind' experiment* where neither the researcher nor the participants know which group they have been allocated to.

Quasi-experimental

All too often, the persons designated as the evaluators are called in too late to establish a truly experimental design. A programme of health or social care may already be up and running with a group of people selected randomly or by some other sampling technique. In this case a non-equivalent or comparison group has to be set up consisting of individuals as closely matched as possible to those in the experimental group. This design lacks the random allocation of people to the two groups which an experimental design can build in. Therefore, what is sometimes called the 'power' of the design is weaker. That is, there is a reduced capacity to detect explanations for the causes of any variations in results. Ideally, those factors which are considered likely to affect outcomes need to be subjected to measurement before the programme begins.

Time-series

This term describes a series of tests or checks at equal intervals before and after a particular programme or package of health of social care is introduced. These are called pre-tests and post-tests. Mid-tests may also be carried out during the course of a programme and can be particularly useful when the programme runs over a long period such as 18 months or more (Fitz-Gibbon and Morris, 1987).

The tests are carried out on the variable(s) which the specific health or social care intervention is designed to influence. These measurements provide a base-line against which post-intervention measurements are compared. Mid-tests made during the course of the formal evaluation check for stability, or variations in any changes recorded.

Example: dependency ratings

A programme has been initiated jointly by a social services department and a community health unit. The main purpose of the scheme is to enable people between the ages of 16 to 60 who have learning disabilities to remain in the community. A specific objective has been stated in these terms:

> **To reduce the dependency levels of at least 70% of those people on the scheme by increasing their contact hours with occupational therapists and community nurses.**

In order to set up the research, a total of 40 people were to be selected from the case records of social workers in one social services department. All cases were given a number which was printed on a piece of paper and placed in a box. The first number drawn out of the box was allocated to the experimental group and the second number to the control group. This process continued until the forty pieces of paper were picked out of the box and each group contained twenty cases.

The next stage was to obtain a dependency rating for each person in the experimental and control groups by administering a validated rating scale. The programme was initially funded for three years.

Scores were recorded from each of the groups, therefore, at the beginning of the programme, at six monthly intervals during the programme, with a final score obtained at the end of the three years. These dependency ratings for each of the groups, obtained by pre-tests, mid-tests and post-tests were examined and subjected to tests of statistical significance in order to discover whether there were differences between the scores obtained by each of the groups. These results would determine whether the programme had been successful according to the criterion of effectiveness defined by the specific programme objective stated above.

Comparative experimental

This type of evaluation design is used to assess the relative effectiveness and efficiency of alternative programme interventions and to measure the impact of intervention compared with non-intervention. The random assignment of individuals to the experimental and control groups is essential. This design is most appropriate for complex programmes which offer a range of different services. In essence, it is an attempt to assess the effect of intervention when a number of different variables are included.

For example, if we were to refer back to the dependency ratings case study, we might wish to introduce other factors into the programme after evaluation has been carried out at the end of the first year of operation. Variation could include:

- reducing or increasing frequency of visits or the number of hours

- confining the next period of twelve months to providing domiciliary support only to persons aged between 45 and 60
- withdrawing visits from occupational therapists or community nurses.

In order to achieve a comparison, the control group could:

- continue to have the same kind and level of service
- be confined to people in the 16–45 age range.

Ethical considerations clearly have to be taken into account in this as with all types of evaluation designs; for example, to what extent does one have the right to withhold a service (which one suspects might be effective) from a particular group?

Crossover

This is a variation of the comparative experimental design. It avoids potential ethical problems related to the withholding of services and the methodological necessity of setting up a control group. In this type of design (Epstein and Tripodi, 1977), Intervention A is given to Group 1 while Intervention B is given to Group 2. After a stipulated period, Intervention A is given to Group 2 and Intervention B to Group 1. Results are then compared.

This design, and all those dealt with above, set out to test for the relationship between an agreed service or set of services and an intended outcome. In effect, these designs are tailored to test hypotheses. In the above example the hypothesis – whether overtly stated or not – is this:

> Intensive contact with occupational therapists and community nurses will substantially reduce the dependency levels of people with learning disabilities.

Technically, the hypothesis which is to be tested is expressed in a negative way, that is that intensive contact will have no effect on dependency levels. This is called the null hypothesis. If there is irrefutable evidence that such contact has reduced dependency levels to a measurably *substantial* degree, then the null hypothesis is said to be disproved. Further attention will be devoted to hypothesis testing later in the chapter. Methodologically, the nub of all these designs lies in the capacity of the evaluator to control variables so that a cause–effect relationship can be discerned between the particular intervention(s) and the measured outcome(s).

Important issues relating to cause–effect designs

1. *Drawing valid inferences*

The purpose of a control group in an evaluation design is that it reduces the possibility of misinterpreting the reasons for certain outcomes. If we refer again to the dependency ratings case study, we could redraft the design to exclude a control group and use a straightforward *before and after* design. In this case, dependency levels of our one group of, say, 40 people would be checked before the domiciliary services were put into effect and checked one year later. What could we deduce from the evidence that in 70% or more of cases dependency levels had improved?

We could only be confident that this benign effect had been directly caused by the particular mode of intervention if all other possible causes could be ruled out as unrelated to the apparent outcome, that is improved dependency levels.

It might be that very similar results could have been obtained with much less domiciliary support, with a different kind of support, or with no such support. Can we tell whether it was the community nursing input or occupational therapy which helped to lower dependency levels? How can we know whether a combination of both these types of support is necessary in order to achieve the intended outcome? The comparative experimental design previously referred to can help to resolve some of these questions.

Only by isolating one particular factor or, in this case, perhaps two factors, can valid inferences be drawn about a relationship between service intervention and outcome.

2. *The Hawthorne effect*

Knowingly being a participant in a new service programme could alter a person's behaviour. This has to be accounted for at the beginning of the process of evaluation design. Ways of minimising the possible effect – known as the *Hawthorne effect* because of the location in the Hawthorne production plant of an experiment in group behaviour and productivity – include the creation of a comparatively large experimental group and control group and a fairly lengthy period of time over which the programme takes place. Alternatively, setting up *blind* or *double-blind experiments* could compensate for the effect, although it has been known for those who receive the placebo to experience greater pain relief than those receiving the actual treatment.

3. *Changing objectives*

Experimental types of design ought not to be conceived as immutable. Relentless adherence to those outcome objectives spelt out at the design stage could prove unrealistic. This is particularly so when the programme to be evaluated runs for a number of years. Objectives, therefore, may change over time. In one sense the notion of 'an outcome' implies terminality, as if – at the end of some arbitrarily designated period – some identifiable change is likely to have occurred. This long-term perspective tends to ignore quite important short-term, perhaps daily, effects of aspects of services upon consumers, upon staff, carers, an organisation or the general public. Close attention within the research design to the monitoring of such possible shifts can be achieved by applying methods of data collection, such as observation techniques, within an experimental design or, indeed, by adapting the research design in such a way that it becomes sensitive to short-term outcomes.

4. *Influences on outcome*

Finally, those evaluating service impact need to be aware that an innovative service, set of services or method of service delivery may affect people other than those who are the focus of the evaluation. For example, the deployment of community nurses and occupational therapists in a relatively intensive domiciliary package of care could positively or negatively affect their performance.

Such innovative programmes could raise or lower staff morale which, in turn, could produce results which are uncharacteristic in terms of the effect such services could normally expect to show on dependency levels.

The crucial task when a design is being formulated is to anticipate those factors or variables which could exert an influence on the outcome to be measured. The unexpected is always a possibility, but careful forethought can help to build into the evaluation design appropriate methods of sifting out red herrings and identifying the real causes of change.

The following set of designs are non-experimental in that they do not attempt to provide cause–effect results, nor do they measure the impact of service intervention on individual participants using a validated measurement scale.

Surveys

Survey designs seek to record people's perceptions, opinions, attitudes and beliefs by means of such devices as interviews, questionnaires and observation. By these means of assembling quantitative and qualitative data, comparisons can be made between consumer expectations of services and those actually received. In short, surveys can afford very interesting insights into personal definitions of *quality*, a point which is extensively dealt with in Chapter 6.

In undertaking a survey the first task is to clearly specify the objectives in precise terms – and this means more than a vague statement of broad intention. It is not enough to say that, for example, the survey is intended to discover the *living conditions of the elderly*. There needs to be a clear indication of what is meant by the term elderly (60+, 65+, 75+, 85+, etc.) and whether living conditions refer to, for example, type of house, age of house, or number of rooms per resident. At this stage the resources available to carry out the survey (that is, time, finance, staff) also need to be considered.

The next stage is to decide whether the population to be studied is to be fully or partially covered. In the latter, and far more usual case, the method of selecting the *sample* has to be determined. This gives rise to a number of questions:

- What type of sample is to be used?
- What is the appropriate sampling unit?
- What sampling frame, if any, is available for the population in question?
- What size sample is required?
- How is non-response to be dealt with?

The quality of the data generated by the survey will depend largely on the quality of the sampling methodology. For example, the sample must be *sufficiently large* to enable relatively precise estimates of the population variable to be made from the sample variable. In addition the sample must be *representative* of the units within the population (that is, if a GP practice wanted to undertake a patient satisfaction survey the sample must be drawn from its patient list rather than the electoral register) and the method of selecting the sample from the population should be by one of the acceptable ways, namely random sampling, systematic sampling, stratified sampling, cluster sampling, multi-stage sampling and quota sampling (for a description of these methods and their relative advantages see, for example, Moser and Kalton, 1977; Dixon and Carr-Hill, 1989). The sample must also produce a *relatively high response rate*, otherwise the data produced may not be representative of the population. For example, in seeking to determine levels of alcohol consumption within a community, there may be a tendency for those with a problem in this area not to respond to a questionnaire asking for weekly consumption levels. It is also necessary to ensure that the *drop-out rate* is minimised, again to ensure that the data is representative of the population being studied.

Used alone or in combination with more quantitative data derived, for example, from experimental types of design, surveys are able to explore areas of highly personal experience which may be invaluable in assisting health and social care organisations to match resources and care packages to individual needs.

Case studies

This type of design has as its focus a particular 'unit'. This may be an individual person, a group of people or an organisation. In health and social care contexts, the individual service user is often the subject of a case study. Case studies allow an in-depth approach to be adopted which is not possible in most other evaluation research designs.

Case studies also serve to counteract possible assumptions that the only valid and, therefore, useful data is that which is founded on large sample numbers and which turns out to be generalisable across other service users and agencies. Individual outcome or process evaluation is an important way of discovering whether health and social services are able to create programmes of care which are sufficiently individualised to be seen as valuable and of benefit by those whom they are intended to help.

'Living-in' designs

We group under this heading those approaches to evaluation which rely on the evaluator becoming very closely connected with the programme participants. Textbooks on social research methods may refer to this design as *ethnomethodology*. In the first few decades of this century, some extremely interesting and influential insights into other cultures were gained by anthropologists who lived amongst the people they were studying. A similar approach was transferred by sociologists to studies of their own culture or sub-cultures such as street gangs and drug users.

There is an element of the experimental in trying to become assimilated into a group of people and something artificial and methodologically problematic in trying to adopt the dual roles of the observed and the observer. Researchers have become wheelchair bound to experience what it is like to be disabled in order to gain answers to questions relating, for example, to prejudice and to the practical facilities available for disabled people in order for them to have access to the same buildings and activities as non-disabled members of society.

People who are not disabled, who are not physically, mentally or financially vulnerable, cannot really enter that other person's world. Nevertheless, by 'living in', experience can be gained which could prove extremely useful, for example, in the preliminary stage of evaluation design by helping to formulate the key issues which are to shape the eventual research design.

Action research, in which the evaluator is in continuous touch with programme participants and provides regular feedback on progress, is a much more visible and more detached form of 'living in'.

Replication studies

A replication study is not a design in its own right, but by repeating previous evaluation studies using the same research design and including highly comparable samples and data collection instruments to those used in the original research, explanations as to why some programmes fail, or succeed, in achieving their stated objectives can be subjected to further scrutiny. The dissemination of replication study findings can make an important contribution to knowledge about the effectiveness of certain service interventions and about the process of evaluation itself.

Evaluation research methods

It is worth emphasising that the quality of the information used in an evaluation depends very largely on the quality of the initial data collected.

Types of data

Data can be classified according to whether they are *quantitative* or *qualitative*. Examples of the former would be the number of clients on a social worker's case-load or the list size of a GP, whilst examples of the latter would include the perceptions of community psychiatric nurses of the impact of the reforms in community care on their professional roles. Quantitative data can be classified into *discrete* data, which are usually 'counts' (for example, the number of patients attending an outpatient clinic) and *continuous* data, measures which lie on a continuum and which, in theory at least, can be recorded to an infinite number of decimal places (for example, distance or temperature). Qualitative data can be classified into *categorical* (or nominal) data (for example, sex, ethnic group) and *ordinal* data, which implies some sort of order (for example, severity of disease, socio-economic group).

Data acquisition

As well as there being different types of data there are different methods of acquiring data. Whilst acknowledging that at some stage all data has to be acquired before being used, it is conventional to distinguish between *primary* data (which has to be collected from original subjects) and *secondary* data (which already exists).

Primary data collection will generally be derived from questionnaires, interviews, observations or a combination of these methods, whilst secondary data will involve the scrutiny of existing reports, records, minutes and statistics. Each method has advantages and disadvantages in terms of time, cost and response rate but it is likely that the 'evaluator', or whoever is responsible for the collection of the data, will have to decide which method(s) to employ. In addition, there may be situations which require the construction of a particular instrument for collecting data. For example, while social workers, community nurses, GPs and the like all have different systems for recording their assessments of patients and clients, the advent of care packages based upon assessment of need may necessitate the construction, adoption or adaptation of standard instruments with which to assess the needs of people. Furthermore, the moves within health and social care to measure aspects associated with quality of life will inevitably result in the development of new scales of measurement. A useful source of material on the procedures involved in the construction of measurement scales is Streiner and Norman (1989).

The role of qualitative evaluation

Qualitative evaluation is generally more useful than quantitative studies when trying to throw light on *relationships* between people within organisations or when developing an understanding of the *perceptions* and *interpretations* that people (staff, patients or clients) have of a particular service. Qualitative data can give an idea of people's intentions and motivations, and the data tends to be 'rich' in the various perspectives revealed. This richness can be extremely useful, but can be very difficult to make sense of, especially if there is a lot of it.

Methods used to collect qualitative data when evaluating services or policies in the health and social care fields include interviews, observation, questionnaires and the scrutiny of relevant documents (for example, reports, minutes, letters, memoranda, white papers and legislation). However, all these methods can also be applied to the collection of quantitative data. The decennial Census, for example, gathers information about the numbers of people living in a particular household, the number of cars available to that household and other quantifiable information. This is done by a census enumerator asking people questions using a structured interview schedule or leaving the schedule for completion by one of the household. Observation sessions could be attempting to chart the frequency of and amount of time spent in the interactions between nursing staff and patients, whilst documents consulted might be entirely statistical.

The collection of qualitative data is often said to be too subjective while quantitative data is much more objective and reliable. However, it is important to remember that quantitative data too is subjective; for example, who decides what is to be counted (or omitted) and how are those decisions made? Whatever kind of data is collected – field notes about people's behaviour or statistics – it needs to be done in a way that, as far as possible, provides information that is valid and reliable. Before considering how to gauge the validity and reliability of data some attention needs to be given to the ways in which data can be collected.

Methods of collecting data

Questionnaires

A questionnaire provides a means of collecting data by framing a set of questions, the responses to which are written on to the questionnaire by the researcher or survey participant. The same set of questions can be put orally to a participant and the responses recorded by the person asking the questions. An *interview* may, therefore, consist of a highly formal set of questions.

Questionnaires are often used to elicit qualitative data, notably people's opinions where, for example, it would be economic in terms of time and resources to do so. Indeed, the self-completed questionnaire might well influence some people to express an opinion more willingly because they might be uneasy in a face-to-face or telephone situation and/or because they are more persuaded that the responses will remain anonymous.

The importance of good questionnaire design cannot be over-emphasised, since the quality and appropriateness of the questions will not only determine the quality of responses but also the quantity of responses. People who find questions ambiguous or difficult to comprehend are less likely to provide answers or, if they do answer the question, the answer may not be appropriate. It is thus essential to test the questionnaire as often as possible prior to its use in a survey. The use of a *pilot study* is essential, where the draft questionnaire is tested on a small group of people, who have the same characteristics as the sample group to be used for the main study.

There are a number of texts which provide useful guidance on questionnaire design (for example, Dixon and Carr-Hill, 1989; Moser and Kalton, 1977; Oppenheim, 1992) and interested readers should consult these for further information. However, a further problem in using questionnaires, especially where the respondent has to complete them and return them to the researcher, is the poor response rate generally produced. There is not a great deal that can be done to remedy this difficulty, other than sending reminder notices, although given the responses generated it is only worth doing this on a few occasions. These issues – of non-response and drop-out rate – may pose particular problems in the interpretation of findings because of the potential *bias* arising from an incomplete set of respondents. For example, non-smokers are more likely to respond to a postal questionnaire dealing with smoking habits.

Interviews

One key aim of an interview in evaluation work is to find out what the interviewee thinks about the service or policy being evaluated. Interviews are particularly useful for accessing information that is otherwise unavailable. For example, one cannot *observe* people's thoughts, nor behaviours which took place in the past.

The interviewer needs to achieve an appropriate balance between maintaining a relaxed and friendly rapport with the interviewee and ensuring that sufficient probing takes place so that the interviewee's first reaction to a question is not necessarily taken as the whole truth: but it is also important to do the probing in a way so as to avoid interviewees becoming unnecessarily guarded or defensive. As with so many things in evaluation work it is not enough simply to go through the motions: interviews need to be undertaken with sensitivity and skill. The interview should not feel like an interrogation: how questions are asked (for example, the tone and pace) is as important as the questions themselves.

Inexperienced interviewers might find it useful to reflect on the different styles used by professional interviewers on various television and radio programmes. For example, the style used by an interviewer in tackling an evasive politician is likely to be more aggressive, though not necessarily more revealing, than a more subtle approach.

Structure of interviews

One of the decisions which needs to be taken before interviewing takes place is on the degree of 'structure' to be used. In 'structured' interviews each interviewee is, as far as possible, asked the same questions in the same way and same sequence without any deviating discussions 'getting in the way'. The advantage of this standardised approach is that it is probably easier to analyse the information gathered. It also makes it easier to replicate the interview with other interviewees in the future by using the same data collection tool and this can help to minimise variations between interviewers where a team of them is being used.

In 'unstructured' or 'guided' interviews, interviewers need to have a clear idea about the purpose and content of the interview, but they should allow and encourage the interviewees to expand on their views. It is more a case of 'following one's nose' to see where the interview goes in a spontaneous and natural way. In such interviews much 'richer' data can be forthcoming, but it is likely to be more difficult to analyse because the 'patterns' in the data are less obvious. A useful and common compromise is the 'semi-structured' interview in which the interviewer has a list of questions to be asked (the 'interview schedule') but in which informants/interviewees are allowed to deviate where the interviewer thinks this is appropriate. In this way unexpected leads may be followed which might reveal useful and relevant information which might be missed by the more 'structured' interview. In open-ended or unstructured interviews in particular it is important not to 'lead' interviewees into expressing views that they do not hold! Patton (1982) expresses this clearly when he points out that the purpose 'is *not* to put things in someone's mind (for example, the interviewer's preconceived categories for organising the world), but rather to access the perspective of the person being interviewed'.

It is possible to combine the various styles of interview. For example, unstructured interviews might be used as an exploratory tool at an early stage to be followed later by more structured interviews from a specific sample of informants.

Probing is a critical skill in interviews. This can be done by asking interviewees to 'elaborate' or 'clarify' an answer or to explain why or how something happened. Longish pauses can also be useful (as long as interviewees do not find this threatening).

A decision is also needed in relation to the capture or recording of interviewees' comments. Should a tape recorder be used or should one rely solely on note taking (tape recording does not remove the need for note taking)? There is no simple answer to this. Each has its advantages and disadvantages. Tape recorders may capture all that is said, but might have an inhibiting effect on interviewees. Tape recordings can also be very time consuming to transcribe and analyse. If a tape recorder is not used it is important that one's notes are written up during and immediately after an interview so that sense can be made of them later.

Observation

Observations can, like interviews, be more or less structured depending on what is appropriate in the particular circumstances. On the one hand, an unstructured approach may be suitable where an external evaluator has entered an organisation for the first time and needs to get a feel for the prevailing culture and procedures as a context for the more detailed evaluation work to come later. Such observations (for example at meetings, case conferences, or committees) can be useful 'sensitising' devices in order to guide the evaluator towards the questions that need to be posed later, possibly in the form of interviews.

On the other hand, where evaluators have a clear idea of what they are looking for (for example in the evaluation of specific organisational processes) a more structured approach may be more appropriate. Such approaches commonly rely on some form of two dimensional matrix. Along one dimension of a matrix there might be the names of the people to be observed, such as the members of a committee. Along the second dimension might be specific behaviours to be observed, for example: introducing novel ideas, assessing suggestions raised by others, keeping the committee's attention on the matter in hand, or being supportive to people who feel under attack.

When one of the people present displays an example of the behaviour in question a tick is placed in the appropriate box. At the end of the meeting an analysis can be undertaken to identify the prevailing styles of behaviour of the various participants. This form of structured evaluation can be useful in assessing, for example, the extent to which Belbin's team roles are being fulfilled (see Chapter 5).

Observations are commonly used in conjunction with interviews and may uncover what people do, as opposed to what they claim they do, and may be participant or non-participant, covert or overt. A useful summary of these forms of observation may be found in Gill and Johnson (1991).

'Participant observation', occurs when the evaluator for all practical purposes becomes a member of the group being observed. This method of data collection is more likely to give the evaluator a deeper insight into 'what is going on' in the group. The participant observer is more likely to feel empathy with (though not necessarily sympathy for) the group being studied and is more likely to uncover the group's 'secrets'. In an interview an informant may keep up a 'front' successfully, a front which may become exposed to the skilled participant observer. However, there is always the danger of the participant observer 'going native': here the observer tends to forget the task of rigorous data collection and abandons reflection and scepticism – the 'participation' has overwhelmed the 'observation'.

'Non-participant observation' is more akin to being a spectator or 'fly on the wall': there is, therefore, likely to be less risk of 'going native'. On the other hand, there is less likelihood of uncovering and understanding 'the cultural underpinnings of subjects' overt behaviours' (Gill and Johnson, 1991).

Should observation be done overtly or covertly? Again there are pros and cons which need to be considered. It may be argued that honesty is always the best policy, but there are occasions when it may be necessary to resort to covert observation. As Gill and Johnson point out there are, generally speaking, two main reasons for using covert observation:

- to avoid the danger of people behaving differently because they know they are being observed (referred to in Chapter 1 as the *Hawthorne* effect); and/or
- to reduce the risk of people refusing the evaluator access (to the processes to be studied) because they do not want an evaluation to be carried out.

However, there are clearly ethical implications for those wishing to use covert methods in evaluations, particularly where confidential matters are being addressed. A strong sense of moral integrity is, therefore, required of the evaluator.

Scrutiny of documents

In the evaluation of health and social care services documentary sources, as stated earlier, are likely to be used in conjunction with other sources of information (possibly interviews and/or observation) rather than as a sole source. Useful documents are likely to include reports, minutes of meetings, policy papers (government white papers or discussion papers within local authorities or health care agencies), Parliamentary debates and evidence to select committees, and legislation.

Documents can be useful in revealing people's stated views, explicit goals and objectives, arguments for and against the introduction of particular services, justifications for specific policies and the statutory frameworks for particular health and social care services. Such information is useful as a template with which to compare the actual implementation and outcomes of particular services.

It is important for evaluators to use a good deal of scepticism in interpreting documents: no document should be taken at face value. Evaluators should ask:

- Who prepared this document, and from what point of view?
- In the case of alleged 'facts' how does the person who prepared the document know? Might the writer be in error? or deliberately misleading?
- Might there be ulterior motives hiding behind the document?
- On what assumptions are statements in the document based?
- Is the distinction between opinions and alleged 'facts' clear?
- To what extent and in what ways is the documentary evidence consistent with other sources of information?
- Does the document rely on secondary evidence from other sources? If so, is it possible to check the accuracy of such secondary reporting?

Documentary evidence can be useful not only for providing answers to particular questions, but also in the preparation of further questions to be followed up by interviews, observation or questionnaires.

The validity and reliability of data

The *validity* of a measurement has been defined as the extent to which it measures what the investigator actually wishes to measure (Abramson, 1990). For example, to find out about a person's social status, data concerning occupation is likely to be more valid than data about the person's hair colour. However, the issue becomes complicated because there are different kinds of validity, for example there is *internal validity*, *external validity*, *content validity*, *predictive validity* and *construct validity*. For a full account of these varieties of validity the reader is advised to consult the appropriate literature on research methods (for example, Gill and Johnson, 1991; Bynner and Stribley, 1979; Walker, 1985; Streiner and Norman, 1989).

In practice, a useful safeguard to achieve as much validity as possible would be to follow these guidelines, based on the work of Runciman (1983) and Miles and Huberman (1984):

- check your conclusions against further sets of data
- practise triangulation (that is, collect different kinds of data about the topic in question from different sources and by different methods to see whether there are any discrepancies between your findings)
- test the feasibility of any recommendations that your research leads you to make
- in order to try to ensure 'authenticity', beware of 'misdescriptions' (Runciman, 1983) such as:

(1) *incompleteness*: e.g. neglect of institutions and practices;
(2) *oversimplification*: e.g. a failure to ask informants for a description in *their* terms which would have resulted in further elaboration
(3) *suppression*; details being excluded which would make the description less favourable to the researcher's own cause
(4) *exaggeration*; descriptions being overstated to make a case for the researcher's own purpose
(5) *ethnocentrism*; assumptions of the researcher's own milieu being inappropriately imposed onto the experiences of members of another

- check for representativeness; for example beware of generalising from particular cases too readily: just because a policy worked well on one hospital it does not necessarily mean that it will work well in all hospitals

- check for researcher effects; for example being co-opted or 'going native' – swallowing the agreed upon or taken-for-granted version of local events
- think about how to weight the evidence; you might decide that information from some informants is likely to be more valid than that from other informants (for example, how knowledgeable, articulate and reflective are your interviewees?)
- be on the look-out for ulterior motives in your informants/interviewees (might they have reasons, possibly quite good reasons, to be less than truthful?)
- look for 'deviant' cases; can your theory or conclusions explain these as well as the 'normal' cases: avoid the temptation to sweep the deviant cases under the carpet!
- think about possible rival explanations to the one you are developing
- get feedback from informants; for example, following interviews and your subsequent writing up of your notes, show the notes to the interviewees to check that you recorded accurately what they said (or meant to say).

Example: pluralistic evaluation

A good example of a qualitative evaluation which uses a number of these guidelines is the evaluation of a psychogeriatric service completed by Smith and Cantley (1985). The evaluators were keen to learn about the service from a number of perspectives. To do this, they adopted a 'pluralistic evaluation' approach: they collected qualitative data by:

- seeking to understand the perspectives of both patients (and their relatives and relatives' support groups) and the various groups of providers of the services;

- using interviews, hospital records and field observations; and
- making (tentative) judgements about the success of the services based on a variety of criteria of 'success'.

Reliability concerns the extent to which repeated measurements (e.g. structured tests and interviews) made on the same material (respondents) by the same measuring instrument (e.g. interview schedule) would achieve the same result (Moser and Kalton, 1977). For example, if a large number of researchers were to study the same phenomenon (using the same method) and their findings turned out to be identical/or highly comparable, then the findings and the research instrument would be regarded as reliable.

However, this can be a problem in qualitative evaluations; to achieve an acceptable degree of reliability evaluations need to be carried out rigorously and systematically, with clear descriptions of the methods of data collection and analysis so that others will be able to replicate the study to compare results.

It can also help if several people are involved in the evaluation, for example perhaps another evaluator or a client of the evaluation. This reduces the risks of relying too much on the interpretations of one individual.

One example of this relates to the increasing use of assessments of Accreditation of Prior Learning (APL) Portfolios (see Chapter 5). To ensure a satisfactory degree of consistency (reliability) in assessment, portfolios can be assessed by different assessors unaware of how others have assessed them. This can help to identify any marked differences in the expectations and standards of different assessors and can suggest where remedial action is needed – possibly for improved assessor training.

There are other considerations to be borne in mind in assessing the reliability and validity of data. For example, once data has been collected it must be *usable*. Reams of unstructured and meandering field notes do not make for easy interpretation and analysis, while another consideration is the way in which the data is used.

Another aspect of the process of verifying the data relates to the *accuracy* or otherwise of the data. For example, according to Woodward and Francis (1988) 'at least one health authority regularly reports men having hysterectomies'.

The role of quantitative evaluation

Unfortunately, the disciplines (statistics and quantitative methods) underlying this particular section are not exactly popular and those who devote their lives to the study of the subject and utilise its techniques are, in the words of Reid and Boore (1987) 'one step up from traffic wardens and one step down from the taxman on the ladder of the public's affections.' However, some comprehension of the role and techniques of statistical and other quantitative techniques will be of considerable value to the evaluator of a programme, which coupled with some computer capabilities will enable vast quantities of data to be processed and analysed in relatively short periods of time. This section of the chapter aims to highlight some of the available quantitative techniques and their uses in data analysis for the evaluation of health and social care programmes.

Data analysis

It is at this stage that many people may feel like 'switching off' or jumping to the next chapter. This would be a shame since many of the apparent complexities surrounding statistics are without foundation. This section dealing with data analysis is broken down into a number of stages.

Stage 1 – Descriptive and summary statistics

The first stage in the process of analysing the data gathered is relatively straightforward. This stage is usually referred to in statistics textbooks as *descriptive and summary statistics*, since it does nothing more than actually describe and summarise the data that has been gathered.

Data can be described in diagrammatic or tabulated format. For example, Table 2.1 illustrates a hypothetical age profile of personnel employed by an NHS trust.

Table 2.1 Hypothetical age profile of NHS trust personnel

Age bracket	Number	Percentage (%)
Under 21	69	5.8
21–30	275	23.2
31–40	391	33.0
41–50	176	14.8
51–60	189	15.9
61 and over	86	7.3
Total	1186	100.0

This data could also be displayed in the form, for example, of a bar chart, or a pie chart, as shown in Figures 2.1 and 2.2.

Figure 2.1 Age profile of employees

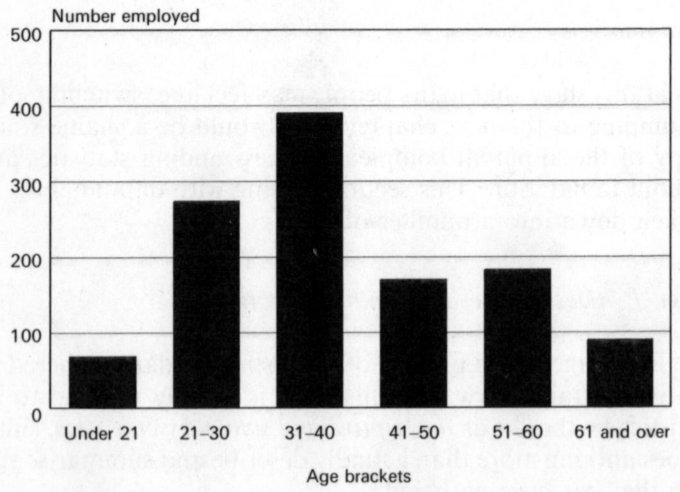

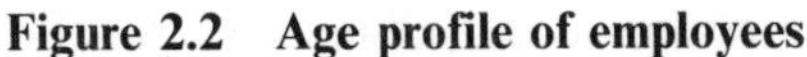

Figure 2.2 Age profile of employees

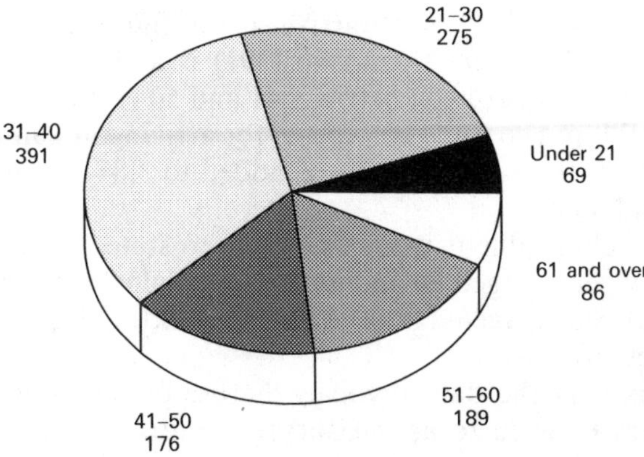

Obviously, there are many other ways in which such data can be presented – see, for example, Reid and Boore (1987) and Woodward and Francis (1988).

In addition, a lot more could be made of such data. For example, additional columns could be inserted into the table to allow for what are termed 'cumulative frequencies and percentages' to be included.

Table 2.2 Age profiles using cumulative frequencies and cumulative percentages

Age bracket	Number	Cumulative frequency	Percentage (%)	Cumulative percentage
Under 21	69	69	5.8	5.8
21–30	275	344	23.2	29.0
31–40	391	735	33.0	62.0
41–50	176	911	14.8	76.8
51–60	189	1100	15.9	92.7
61 and over	86	1186	7.3	100

In order to arrive at the cumulative frequency column the number aged under 21 (69) is added to the number aged between 21 and 30 (275) to arrive at the figure of 344. The number aged between 31 and 40 (391) is added to produce 735, and the number aged between 41 and 50 (176) is added to produce 911 and so on. The process for arriving at cumulative percentage is the same – 23.2% is added to 5.8% to arrive at 29.0% and so on.

From such a table it is then possible to state, for example, how many people aged 50 and under are employed by the trust (911) and what percentage of the total workforce are aged 40 and under (62%).

Summarising the data involves the use of ratios, averages (sometimes referred to as measures of central tendency) and measures of dispersion.

A *ratio* is the general term for rates, proportions, percentages and ratios themselves. A *rate* is an expression of one variable in terms of a unit of another variable, for example, number of nurses per GP practice.

Proportions and *percentages* compare a part with the whole; for example, the proportion of people aged 61 and over employed in the NHS trust is the part (86) divided by the whole (1186), that is

$$86/1186 = 0.073.$$

Percentages are simply proportions multiplied by 100. Therefore, the percentage of people aged 61 and over employed in the NHS trust is

$$0.07 \times 100 = 7.3\%.$$

Ratios compare the two parts, which constitute the whole. In other words, the ratio of people aged 61 and over employed in the NHS trust to those aged 60 and less is

$$86/1100 = 0.078$$

which can also be expressed as 86:1100 or 1:12.79.

Averages or *measures of central tendency* can take one of three basic types (for a discussion of others – for example, geometric mean, weighted average, moving average – see Woodward and Francis, 1988). These are the:

- *Mean* (sometimes referred to as the arithmetic mean), which is the sum (or total) of the data divided by the number of values in the data.
- *Median*, which is the mid-point of the data set, that is half of the values are less than the median and half are greater.
- *Mode*, which is the most frequently occurring value in the data set.

The fact that these averages are different means that they may produce different results. In order to illustrate this point data on length of stay in hospital contained in Table 2.3 will be utilised.

Table 2.3 Data on length of hospital stay

Length of stay (days)	Number
2	12
3	15
4	9
5	10
6	6
17	1
25	1
30	1
Total	55

In order to calculate the mean, the sum of the data is divided by the number of values, that is

$$(2 \times 12) + (3 \times 15) + (4 \times 9) + (5 \times 10) + (6 \times 6) + (17 \times 1) + (25 \times 1) + (30 \times 1)/55$$

which is,

$$24 + 45 + 36 + 50 + 36 + 17 + 25 + 30/55$$

that is,

$$263/55 = \underline{\underline{4.78}}$$

In order to calculate the median the numbers need to be presented in order, that is

2, 2, 2, 2, 2, 2, 2, 2, 2, 2, 2, 2, 3, 3, 3, 3, 3, 3, 3,
3, 3, 3, 3, 3, 3, 3, 3, 4, 4, 4, 4, 4, 4, 4, 4, 4, 5, 5,
5, 5, 5, 5, 5, 5, 5, 5, 6, 6, 6, 6, 6, 6, 17, 25, 30

There are 55 values of data and therefore the middle value – the median – will be the 28th, with 27 values below and 27 values above. (In cases where there are an even number of data values the two middle values are taken and the mean of these is the median.) The 28th value (in ascending order) is the first of the nine 4s and therefore the median is equal to 4.

The mode is relatively straightforward to identify, being the most frequently occurring value, which in Table 2.3 is 3.

In the above data set there are three possible average values:

- The mean of 4.78
- The median of 4
- The mode of 3

It is generally recommended that the mean is used as the average, unless there are extreme values in the data set, which distort the mean and result in a skewed distribution, when the median should be used. The mode is not usually recommended. However, it should be made quite clear which method is used as a measure of the average or central tendency.

Measures of dispersion are necessary as summary statistics because averages cannot, in themselves, summarise all of the characteristics of the data set. It is necessary to include an indicator of the extent to which the data is dispersed around the measure of central tendency, a function which measures of dispersion fulfil.

The *range* is the simplest measure of dispersion because it is simply the difference between the smallest and the largest value in the data set. In the data set above, the range is 28 days, that is the difference between 30 days and 2 days.

The most widely used measure of dispersion is the *standard deviation*. This considers the extent of the deviation between the data values and the average. There are five steps in its calculation.

The data set used in calculating the mean and the median will again be utilised to illustrate the five steps.

2, 2, 2, 2, 2, 2, 2, 2, 2, 2, 2, 2, 3, 3, 3, 3, 3, 3, 3,
3, 3, 3, 3, 3, 3, 3, 3, 4, 4, 4, 4, 4, 4, 4, 4, 4, 5, 5,
5, 5, 5, 5, 5, 5, 5, 5, 6, 6, 6, 6, 6, 6, 17, 25, 30

The first step is to calculate the deviation between each data value and the mean. Since we know that the mean is 4.78 it is a mechanical exercise to subtract the mean from each of the above values. For example, using the first data value (2),

$$2 - 4.78 = -2.78$$

Repeating this for each data value produces

–2.78, –2.78, –2.78, –2.78, –2.78, –2.78, –2.78, –2.78, –2.78,
–2.78, –2.78, –2.78, –1.78, –1.78, –1.78, –1.78, –1.78, –1.78,
–1.78, –1.78, –1.78, –1.78, –1.78, –1.78, –1.78, –1.78, –1.78,
–0.78, –0.78, –0.78, –0.78, –0.78, –0.78, –0.78, –0.78, –0.78,
0.22, 0.22, 0.22, 0.22, 0.22, 0.22, 0.22, 0.22, 0.22,
0.22, 1.22, 1.22, 1.22, 1.22, 1.22, 1.22, 12.22, 20.22,
25.22

The second step is to square each of these deviations, since if they were simply totalled the result would be equal to 0.

7.73, 7.73, 7.73, 7.73, 7.73, 7.73, 7.73,
7.73, 7.73, 7.73, 7.73, 7.73, 3.17, 3.17,
3.17, 3.17, 3.17, 3.17, 3.17, 3.17, 3.17,
3.17, 3.17, 3.17, 3.17, 3.17, 3.17, 0.61,
0.61, 0.61, 0.61, 0.61, 0.61, 0.61, 0.61,
0.61, 0.048, 0.048, 0.048, 0.048, 0.048, 0.048,
0.048, 0.048, 0.048, 0.048, 1.49, 1.49, 1.49,
1.49, 1.49, 1.49, 149.33, 408.85, 636.05

Thirdly, the sum of the above squared deviations is found. The result is equal to 1349.45.

The fourth stage is to divide this by the number of data values less 1 (because the differences have what is termed n – 1 *degrees of freedom*). In this case there are 55 data values, so the denominator to use is 54. This result produces what is known as the *variance* and is equal to

1349.45/54 = 24.99

The final step is to find the square root of 24.99, which is (after rounding up the decimal places) equal to 5.

What is meant by the 'standard deviation'? The standard deviation provides an indicator of the degree of dispersion in the variable. In the data relating to length of stay in hospital it is equal to 5. The greater the magnitude of the standard deviation the greater is the range of values within the distribution. The standard deviation is also linked to the concept of the *normal distribution*, which has a bell shape and is symmetrical. It arises when a variable is measured for a large number of basically identical objects (such as the height of people) and when variation may be caused by a number of different factors. The normal distribution displays certain properties which are extremely useful in analysing data. The normal distribution in Figure 2.3 below has the arithmetic mean at its mid (also the highest) point and is divided into three standard deviations each side of this mid point. It is possible to show that approximately 68% of the area of a normal distribution lies between −1 and +1 standard deviations, that is within 1 standard deviation either side of the mean; approximately 96% of *all* possible values lie within 2 standard deviations either side of the mean; and, approximately 99.7% of *all* possible values lie within 3 standard deviations either side of the mean.

Figure 2.3 The normal distribution

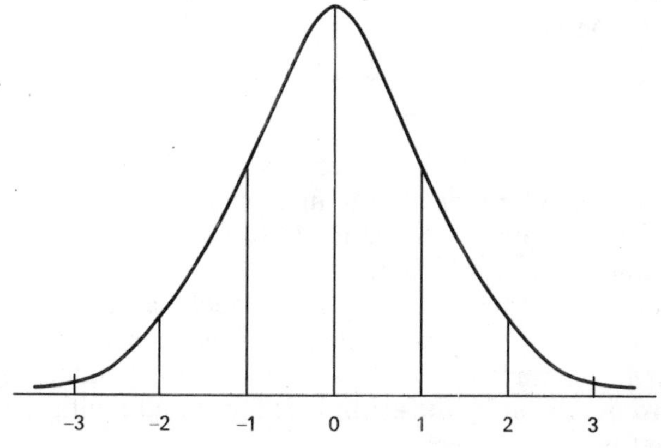

Example: systolic blood pressure

Suppose we knew that the systolic blood pressure of a group of 200 people randomly chosen to be engaged in a clinical trial is normally distributed with an arithmetic mean of 130 mmhg and a standard deviation of 18.

Using the properties of the normal distribution we could state that:

- approximately 68% have systolic blood pressure between [130 – 18] and [130 + 18] mmhg, that is between

  112 and 148 mmhg
- approximately 96% have systolic blood pressure between [130 – (2 × 18)] and [130 + (2 × 18)] mmhg, that is between

  94 and 166 mmhg
- approximately 99.7% have systolic blood pressure between [130 – (3 × 18)] and [130 + (3 × 18)] mmhg, that is between

  76 and 184 mmhg

The first statement is equivalent to stating that *the probability that a randomly selected sample will have a systolic blood pressure between 112 and 148 mmhg is either 0.68 or 68%.*

Relative dispersion It is sometimes useful to combine the mean and standard deviation in a single entity, especially where comparisons are to be made between data sets, where one contains values which are generally much larger than the other data set, thus resulting in a much larger mean and standard deviation. This single entity is referred to as the *coefficient of variation* and is arrived at by dividing the standard deviation by the arithmetic mean and multiplying by 100, that is

$$\text{Coefficient of variation} = \frac{\text{Standard deviation}}{\text{Arithmetic mean}} \times 100$$

However, in just the same way as the mean may not be the most appropriate measure of central tendency when the data is *skewed* (that is, not symmetrical), the same applies to the standard deviation as a measure of dispersion. In Table 2.3 on lengths of stay in hospital above, the data is skewed in that the distributions are not symmetrical and thus the standard deviation is not very helpful. In such cases a more appropriate measure is the *quartile deviation* (also known as the *semi-interquartile range*). Quartiles are an extension of the methodology of the median. Instead of dividing the data set into two parts it is divided into four parts, resulting in three quartiles. The *quartile deviation* is half the distance between the first and third quartiles.

For a much fuller discussion of these and additional aspects of descriptive and summary statistics see one of the many statistics textbooks available, for example, Campbell and Machin (1990); Reid and Boore (1987) and Woodward and Francis (1988).

Stage 2 – Estimation

The second stage of data analysis to be considered is the ability to generalise from findings produced by means of sampling to the population from which the sample was drawn.

The use of *confidence intervals* enables, for example, the proportion of GPs suffering from some degree of stress to be estimated from the findings of a survey carried out amongst a sample of GPs. It is impossible to be absolutely sure of the population value but this technique enables the analyst to determine with some degree of confidence (expressed in percentage terms) the range of values within which the population value would lie.

Example: GP stress

A survey of 200 GPs produced evidence that 72% of them had suffered from some stress related problems over the previous 12 months. Whilst recognising the limitations of such a statement, by using *confidence intervals* it is possible to translate the sample percentage into at least an indication of what the *population percentage* is likely to be.

From the normal distribution we know that 95% of all values lie between 1.96 standard deviations either side of the mean (see Figure 2.3). If it were possible to produce findings relating to the percentage who had suffered from stress problems from all possible samples of 200 GPs from the population of GPs the resultant distribution of sample percentages would result in a normal distribution. However, there is no need to contemplate this because the notion of confidence intervals allows the single sample percentage to be used as the indicator, as can be seen from the following formula:

$$P = p \pm 1.96\sqrt{(p \times q)/n}$$

where P is the population percentage
p is the sample percentage
q is (100 – sample percentage)
n is the number in the sample

Therefore, in the case of GPs,

$$P = 72 \pm 1.96\sqrt{(72 \times 28)/200}$$

which results in the population *percentage* being between 66% and 78%.

However, if there had been 2000 GPs in the sample rather than 200 the *population percentage* would be between 71% and 73%, highlighting the obvious attraction of having relatively large numbers in the sample.

Stage 3 – Testing hypotheses

The third stage involves the use of data in confirming or rejecting hypotheses. There are a number of statistical tests, the choice of which and the way in which they are used is dependent upon the type of data, the quantity of data and the extent to which incorrect conclusions may be tolerated. The first two of these factors, type and quantity of data, would dictate whether a *parametric* or *non-parametric* statistical test is used. If the distribution of the data is not *normal*, that is, it is not *bell-shaped* as in Figure 2.4a, but skewed to the left or the right, as in Figure 2.4b and Figure 2.4c, and the sample size is relatively small it is necessary to use a non-parametric test.

Other situations which dictate the use of non-parametric tests are when the data is categorical or ordinal, for example, the use of rankings. The philosophy underlying both parametric and non-parametric tests is exactly the same. The rationale for distinguishing between them is that when the data does not conform to certain conditions, as highlighted above, non-parametric tests produce superior results; when the data does conform to these conditions parametric tests provide superior results.

Figure 2.4a Distribution of data: normal

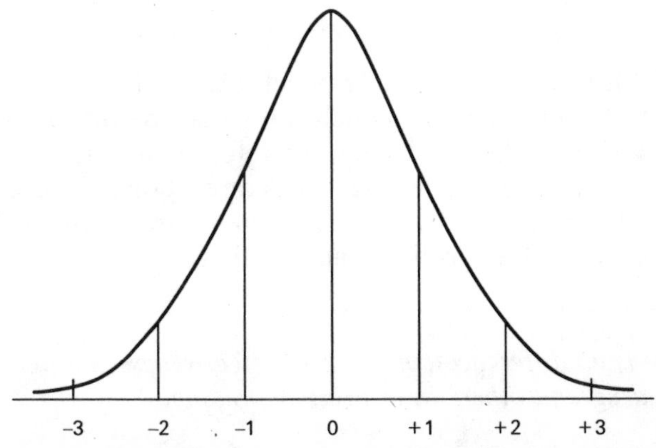

Figure 2.4b Distribution: skewed to the left

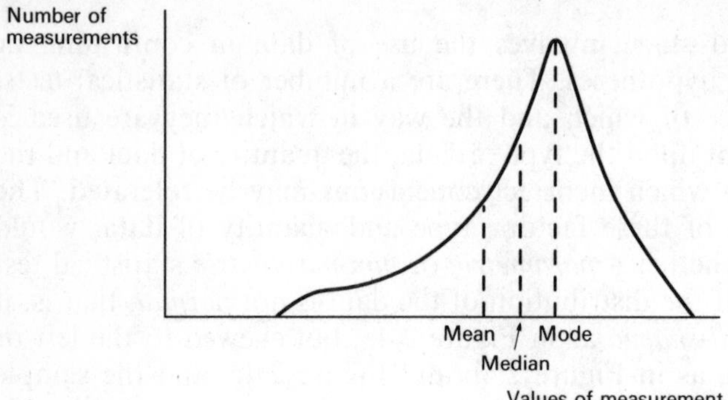

Figure 2.4c Distribution: skewed to the right

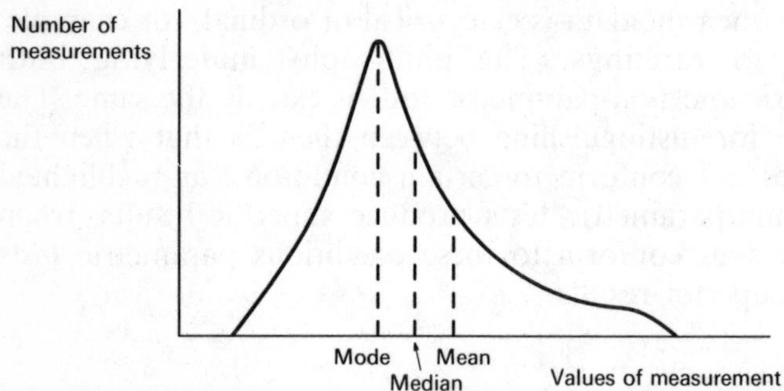

The third factor influencing which test to use concerns the extent to which incorrect conclusions may be drawn on the basis of the results produced. As referred to earlier in the chapter, in hypothesis testing it is conventional to speak in terms of the *null hypothesis* and the *alternative hypothesis*. For example, the null hypothesis may be that

> *there is no difference (in terms of effectiveness) between a new drug and others in treating depression*

whilst the alternative hypothesis is that

> *there is a difference (in terms of effectiveness) between a new drug and others in treating depression*

Therefore in seeking to confirm the alternative hypothesis, the null hypothesis is simultaneously rejected. Alternatively, in rejecting the alternative hypothesis the null hypothesis is confirmed. However, it is impossible to be 100% accurate and one of two types of error may be made. The first type (known as Type I error) is to *reject* the null hypothesis when it is *true*. The second type of error (Type II error) is of *failing* to reject the null hypothesis when it is *actually false*. The probability of having a Type I error is known as the *significance level* and is expressed in percentage terms. It is usual to adopt a 5% significance level (which means that in 95% of cases it is appropriate to reject the null hypothesis, or to put it another way the probability of it happening by chance is 5 in 100 or 1 in 20), although for situations involving drug testing and the like, a very small significance level should be used, because of the potentially disastrous consequences of using unsuitable drugs.

It is not usual to express the probability of having a Type II error, but rather the *power of the test*, which is the probability of rejecting the null hypothesis when the alternative hypothesis is true. (It is equal to (1 – probability of a Type II error).)

Stage 4 – Relationships

The fourth stage is entitled 'relationships' since it examines whether or not there is any association between two or more variables and the strength of such relationships. For example, the *chi-squared* test could be utilised to determine whether there is any significant relationship between social class and patients' satisfaction with their GPs.

In addition, a *correlation coefficient* can indicate the strength of the relationship between, for example, children's diet and level of IQ, whilst *regression analysis* could indicate the nature and extent of the relationship between, for example, the incidence of heart disease and level of smoking, diet, degree of stress, weight, extent of exercise, and so on.

The formulae for undertaking regression and correlation are rather formidable for the mathematically disinclined, but as with all the above stages, the advent of computer technology has removed much of the tedium and heartache associated with 'number-crunching'. Computer spreadsheet packages contain some of the more straightforward statistical processes required to arrive at such results whilst other packages, such as SPSS/PC+, merely require a series of fairly simple commands to produce such results within a matter of seconds.

Stage 5 – Other techniques

Other quantitative techniques can also be of use in the context of evaluating health and social care. For example, the use of investment appraisal, from the world of financial management, is described in Chapter 4, where the aim is to arrive at the most efficient use of limited resources. Furthermore, the discipline of Operational Research originated with the aim of solving problems in business, industry, government and the public sector from a scientific perspective and therefore the methodologies of the discipline (for example, forecasting, queueing, programming, simulation, network analysis, theory of games) can also be brought into use in the process of evaluation in the field of health and social care. For example, the most efficient way of operating a hospital out-patient department may be evaluated using aspects of queueing theory, whilst network analysis can provide a clear picture of the time needed to be devoted to reorganisation of the home care services in a local authority.

Summary and checklist

This chapter has sought to highlight the preliminary steps in undertaking any evaluation. The choice of design most appropriate for the investigation must be made carefully otherwise the data generated and the findings produced may be totally inappropriate. Decisions have to be made as to the sort of data that is required, how it is going to be collected, whether it is valid and reliable and how it is going to be analysed. These choices and decisions have to be made before any actual evaluation can take place and the following checklist (based on Patton, 1987) should be of help in this planning stage.

1 Who are the primary stakeholders for the evaluation?
2 What is the purpose of the evaluation?
3 What approach, model or framework will be used to provide direction for the evaluation?
4 What are the main evaluation questions or issues?
5 What political and ethical considerations need to be taken into account?
6 By what standards and criteria will the evaluation be judged?
7 What resources are available for the evaluation?
8 Who should carry out the evaluation?
9 What will be the method(s) of enquiry?
10 What sort of data is needed?
11 How is the data to be analysed?
12 What kind of analysis will be carried out?
13 What resources are needed for the analysis?
14 What will be the sampling strategy?
15 What comparisons, if any, will be made?
16 What research instruments will be used?
17 What level of accuracy of data is required and how will it be achieved?
18 How will the data be checked for its validity and reliability?
19 How will the findings be presented?
20 To whom are the findings going to be made available?

References

Abramson, J. H. (1990) *Survey Methods in Community Medicine*, Churchill Livingstone, London.

Bynner, J. and Stribley, K. M. (eds) (1979) *Social Research: principles and procedures*, Longman in association with the Open University Press, Milton Keynes.

Campbell, M. J. and Machin, D. (1990) *Medical Statistics: a commonsense approach*, Wiley, Chichester.

Dixon, P. and Carr-Hill, R. (1989) *Customer Feedback Surveys – an introduction to survey methods*, Booklet 2 in series entitled 'The NHS and its Customers', Centre for Health Economics, University of York.

Epstein, I. and Tripodi, T. (1977) *Research Techniques for Program Planning*, Columbia University Press, New York.

Fitz-Gibbon, C. T. and Morris, L. L. (1987) *How to Design a Program Evaluation*, Sage, Beverly Hills.

Gill, J. and Johnson, P. (1991) *Research Methods for Managers*, Paul Chapman, London.

Miles, M. and Huberman, A. (1984) *Qualitative Data Analysis: a sourcebook of new methods*, Sage, London.

Moser, C. and Kalton, G. (1977) *Survey Methods in Social Investigation*, Heinemann, London.

Oppenheim, A. N. (1992) *Questionnaire Design and Attitude Measurement*, Pinter, London.

Patton, M. Q. (1982) *Practical Evaluation*, Sage, London.

Reid, N. G. and Boore, J. R. P. (1987) *Research Methods and Statistics in Health Care*, Arnold, London.

Runciman, W. (1983) *A Treatise on Social Theory: the methodology of social theory*, Cambridge University Press.

Smith, G. and Cantley, C. (1985) 'Policy evaluation: the use of varied data in a study of a psychogeriatric service', in Walker (ed.) (1985).

Streiner, D. L. and Norman, G. R. (1989) *Health Measurement Scales: a practical guide to their development and use*, Oxford University Press.

Walker, R. (ed.) (1985) *Applied Qualitative Research*, Gower, London.

Woodward, M. and Francis, L. M. A. (1988) *Statistics for Health Management and Research*, Arnold, London.

3

Evaluating Effectiveness

What is effectiveness?

'Effectiveness' concerns the extent to which stated goals and objectives are being achieved. Both 'goals' and 'objectives' refer to the desired outcomes of a particular policy, programme or service. There are other labels which are also sometimes used to refer to the same idea, e.g. aim, purpose, mission, or target.

The main distinction between these various concepts is the extent to which they are general or specific. For example, a general goal or aim might be the desired end of maximising the health of a given population. This is probably a worthwhile goal but it is rather vague, e.g. how is the health to be assessed or measured? And by when is the goal to be achieved? An objective or target, on the other hand, would be more specific, e.g. 'to reduce the infection rate following a particular kind of operation in this hospital by x% by the end of this year'.

Why is 'effectiveness' and the specification of clear objectives important?

In planning, implementing and evaluating health and social care programmes, professionals and managers need to have clear ideas about what the programmes are setting out to achieve. Without such clarity it is unlikely that the goals and the intended purposes of a service will be achieved; indeed, no one will ever know whether they are being achieved or not!

Because of the way we have defined 'effectiveness' it is clearly necessary for people in organisations to be explicit about their objectives if effectiveness is to be used as an evaluative criterion. In this sense the use of 'effectiveness' in evaluating performance and the setting of explicit objectives are two inseparable processes. Being clear and explicit about objectives is a precondition for assessing the effectiveness of a service. There are also a number of other reasons why it is important for managers and professionals to have clear objectives. Some of these reasons are as follows.

1 If an objective is spelt out loud and clear it is more likely to be abandoned! It is unhealthy for organisations to continue to do things 'because we've always done it like this'. The more explicit the organisation's objectives are the more likely it is that they will, from time to time, be reviewed and challenged. Although this can be an uncomfortable experience, especially when it happens too frequently, it does mean that the organisation is more likely to be responsive to the changing needs of the community.

2 Being explicit about objectives can help managers and professionals to discuss the priorities which should take the lion's share of the budget in a particular time period. The staff involved are unlikely to agree on all the priorities but at least they can have a useful dialogue if the candidates for priority spending have been spelt out clearly.

3 Staff appraisal or individual performance review is a difficult task to perform systematically and effectively. The task can be made easier by ensuring that all members of staff have agreed explicit objectives against which their performance will be judged. This is likely to be a more satisfactory yardstick than rough and ready criteria like 'Do their faces fit?' or 'Are they rocking the boat too much?' Furthermore, explicit objectives are helpful in the evaluation of the performance of whole organisations, policies and services.

4 People who have a clear idea about what is expected of them are likely to be more strongly motivated than.those who are unclear about their role. Explicit objectives can, therefore, act as a motivator for better performance. Clear objectives also help people to feel a sense of achievement when they perform well.

5 If objectives are communicated to colleagues within the organisation, interdepartmental coordination can be achieved and maintained. Such communication is only possible if objectives have been made explicit.

It is for these reasons that managers and professionals need to take the trouble to be explicit about what they are trying to achieve. There are difficulties in achieving agreement on objectives because, more often than not, there will be disagreements between people about what the organisation should be setting out to achieve and about the methods to be used. Nevertheless, we believe that managers and professionals should seek to achieve as much agreement as possible.

How to formulate objectives in order to assess effectiveness

As we have pointed out elsewhere (Palfrey *et al.*, 1992), objectives should be targeted at meeting the needs of clients, and wherever possible, should be:

1 *Explicit*: i.e. they should be discussed and written down rather than implicit; if objectives are merely assumed or taken for granted, they are less likely to be the result of deliberate or sensible planning.

2 *Specific* (rather than general or vague): e.g. 'to provide at least one visit per day to every client (within a particular category)' is more specific than 'to provide support for clients in need'; the trouble with general goals – if not accompanied by specific objectives – is that they leave too much scope for

uncertainty and interpretation. It is then rarely clear whether goals are being achieved.

3 *Measurable*: some aspects of quality of care might be very difficult or impossible to measure, but many relevant measures are available (e.g. the numbers of clients in various categories receiving particular kinds of service).

4 *Scheduled*: people should know the date by which it is intended that the objectives will be achieved; e.g. 'to increase the number of clients receiving a specific service by x% by 30 April 199X'; if an objective does not have a 'due date' there is unlikely to be much sense of urgency, and people are then likely to work towards achieving the objective 'when we have time'.

5 *Prioritised*; it is likely that pressure on resources will make it necessary to decide the order of importance of the objectives – however difficult this might seem; we believe that the task of priority-setting is one of the most important elements in management: without it, people are more likely to spend valuable time and money on chasing relatively unimportant targets.

6 '*Owned*' by a particular worker, team or department – so that people will feel more committed to achieving the objectives, and will know that they may be held accountable in due course; one way to achieve this sense of ownership is to make sure that the people who are expected to achieve the objectives themselves have a significant influence on the setting of the objectives. This idea of participative management is commonly written about and managers often pay lip service to it – but the important thing is for staff to feel that they are indeed involved in key decision-making.

7 *Related to each other* in such a way that the number of conflicting or contradictory objectives throughout the organisation is minimised. If one part of the organisation is trying to reduce the costs of providing a service at the same time as another part is trying to improve the quality of the service, this is

not impossible (it could be achieved by finding more efficient ways of doing things) but it commonly creates tensions and conflicts within the organisation. As far as possible objectives should not be incompatible with each other.

8 *Communicated* to all those who need to know, not only when the objectives are set but also, if relevant, when they are modified, and when they are achieved.

Examples of the setting of objectives in relation to health and social care policies

The Merrison Report

In 1979, the Report of the Royal Commission on the NHS (the Merrison Report) stated the objectives which the NHS could be expected to achieve (1979, pp. 9–12). They were as follows:

(a) To encourage and assist individuals to remain healthy.
(b) To ensure equal entitlement to services.
(c) To provide a broad range of services of high standard.
(d) To ensure equal access to these services.
(e) To provide health care free at time of use.
(f) To satisfy reasonable public expectations for health care.
(g) To provide a national service responsive to local needs.

It is interesting to consider these objectives in relation to the themes discussed in this chapter. For example:

- To what extent are the seven objectives (a)–(g) above specified in accordance with the guidance offered earlier in this chapter?
- To what extent and in what ways have the objectives been achieved?
- How easy or difficult is it to decide whether or not the objectives have been achieved?
- In what ways might the objectives be in conflict with other goals of the NHS, e.g. to achieve 'value for money'?
- To what extent are the objectives still relevant in the NHS of the 1990s (e.g. with the reforms based on the 1989 White Paper *Working for Patients*)? In Sheaff's judgement (1991, p. 2) objectives (c), (e), (f) and (g) are still recognised as important.

The objectives do not generally satisfy the guidance in this chapter. For example, they are not very specific, not measurable and not scheduled. Nevertheless they remain one of the few attempts to offer objectives for the NHS as a whole, and they comprise a number of values which are commonly held in relation to the service. The problem is that the objectives' lack of specificity makes it difficult to judge the extent to which they have been achieved.

Other official prescriptions

The need for health and social care agencies to have explicit objectives has been emphasised in a number of documents from government and other agencies in recent years. For example:

- social service authorities are expected to prepare social/community care plans
- health and local authorities are expected to develop community services in order to help vulnerable

people cope as independently as possible in their own homes

- the 1992 White Paper, *The Health of the Nation*, sets targets for a healthier population (Department of Health, 1992)
- in 1991, the government's proposals for a Citizen's Charter were based largely on the idea of public sector organisations having specific targets or objectives (including health authorities in relation to waiting times), with citizens being able to claim compensation where organisations fail to meet the targets
- the World Health Organisation's *Health for All* objectives.

Corporate planning

For several decades, local authorities and other organisations have been urged to adopt a more rational and corporate approach to planning and evaluating their services. The kind of corporate planning which has been advocated has the following features:

1 the determination of goals and objectives – in relation to various client groups and their needs/problems;
2 the evaluation of the alternative means costs, benefits, and distribution thereof of achieving the objectives
3 the selection of the most promising means
4 the setting of specific targets
5 implementation
6 evaluation and review.

The setting of objectives is clearly an important part of this process, and readers are invited to reflect on the extent to which their own organisations follow this kind of process. In doing this it is not enough to look at organisation structures (e.g. the existence of Policy Committees and Management Teams); it is necessary to look at what is actually done – does the setting of objectives follow the guidance offered in this chapter?

Specific targets

Managers and professionals have much to gain by having specific targets to achieve. Sometimes targets or measurable objectives are used as a part of staff appraisal or individual performance review systems. Examples of targets might include:

(a) meeting important deadlines
(b) minimising the number of errors made
(c) minimising the number of complaints
(d) minimising delays
(e) adherence to specified quality standards
(f) keeping within budgetary limits
(g) productivity levels (e.g. the number of meals on wheels, or other units of work, per employee hour)
(h) ensuring that the necessary training is provided for specific staff
(i) ensuring that work processes are reviewed regularly to see whether more efficient systems can be developed
(j) ensuring that staffs' job descriptions are reviewed regularly
(k) minimising levels of staff turnover, absenteeism and sickness
(l) minimising poor time-keeping
(m) minimising accidents at work.

In these examples it is not difficult to see that one could quantify the targets where appropriate. Not all of the measures are necessarily relevant to all work situations but they serve as examples of targets that managers in a particular department might consider.

Alternatively, targets might be a part of a performance indicator package (see Chapter 1) or may be specified in relation to identifiable health gain, e.g. to reduce deaths from respiratory disease below age 65 by 20% by 2002 (Welsh Office NHS Directorate, 1992).

All these initiatives require local authorities, health care agencies and/or independent bodies to develop specific objectives for their areas so that judgements can subsequently be made about the organisation's effectiveness. The setting of the objectives will not be a panacea for organisational performance, and a number of the difficulties outlined earlier in this chapter are likely to limit the usefulness of the exercises. However, the process of objective-setting can serve as a useful discipline for managers and professionals, will help in the process of deciding priorities, and will subsequently enable people to assess the effectiveness of the policies or services in question.

An exercise in the formulation of objectives: the case of the emerging self-governing trust

In 1991, the Cambrian Community Health Unit, within a (fictional) midlands health authority, became a self-governing trust within the NHS. Quite soon after the confirmation that the trust's application for self-governing status was to be granted, the Unit General Manager (now to be called the Chief Executive) came under increasing pressure to improve the unit's planning capacity.

As a 'provider' within the reformed NHS, the unit needed to develop a very clear idea of the services to which it wanted to give priority and to have a set of explicit objectives for the emerging business plan being prepared by the unit's planning department.

The chief executive wrote to all the departmental heads asking each of them to prepare a statement of objectives against which performance could be evaluated in future, the statement to be reviewed on an annual basis. The request met with a wide range of responses. At one extreme, the planning department itself prepared a clear and specific set of measurable objectives. On the other hand, some of the health care professions were sceptical about the value of trying to have specific objectives when dealing with intangible issues like the quality of care and the difficulties of assessing outcomes of treatments.

It was decided by the Trust's Managing Board that in future, departmental budgets would depend on the extent to which each department could demonstrate its effectiveness against explicit objectives.

If you were one of the health care professionals, *how would you respond* to the chief executive's request for a statement of your department's specific objectives?

The problems involved in using 'effectiveness' as an evaluative criterion

The first difficulty is that organisational and professional objectives are commonly specified only in vague and general terms, e.g. 'to improve care for our clients'. In many other cases, no objectives are specified at all.

Secondly, being effective is not the same as providing a good service which leads to useful outcomes. If objectives are specified or selected inappropriately, an organisation could be effective in promoting inappropriate policies. The provision of high rise dwellings for some groups of people and the institutionalisation of elderly people might be examples of this phenomenon.

The third limitation is that effectiveness takes no account of the costs of achieving objectives. In assessing performance, one needs to take account of the resources used as well as the objectives being achieved.

Fourthly, the achievement of specified objectives might lead to unfortunate side-effects in related areas of policy; e.g. reducing the time that patients occupy hospital beds can release much needed beds but can also place great pressure on overstretched community services, with a possible decline in the level of care available to some groups in the community.

A fifth problem concerns the need to understand the links between a policy or 'intervention' in health or social care and what appears to be the outcome of that intervention. For example, if mortality rates decline a year after an increase in expenditure on medical and nursing establishment, it would be unwise to assume that it was the increase in expenditure that caused the reduction in mortality.

The extent to which one variable effects a change in another variable is usually a complex question in health and social care. Mortality rates are affected by a wide variety of factors, including environmental conditions, diet and personal behaviour patterns (e.g. cigarette smoking and degree of physical exercise). The increased expenditure might have had a part to play, but to say that it 'caused' the improved mortality statistics is not warranted.

Despite these difficulties, we believe that it is important for managers and professionals to develop explicit objectives. They are a prerequisite for effective performance.

Summary and checklist

The main argument in this chapter is that in the interests of meeting the needs of the intended recipients of a health or social care service, the organisations involved (be they health or local authorities, voluntary or private sector organisations or other agencies) need to be clear about what they are trying to achieve, i.e. their objectives. This clarity is a precondition for evaluating the extent to which the organisations are being effective – achieving that which they set out to achieve.

Managers and professional could usefully work their way through the following checklist in relation to their own organisation, department or service.

1 Is there a clear and agreed view about what the department is trying to achieve?

2 Are the most influential managers and professionals committed to these objectives?

3 Are the objectives:

(a) Explicit?
(b) Specific?
(c) Measurable?
(d) Scheduled?
(e) Prioritised?
(f) 'Owned' by the managers and professionals involved?
(g) Related to each other?
(h) Communicated to all who need to know?

4 What information will need to be collected in order to judge the extent to which the objectives have been achieved in due course? Who will carry out this evaluation, and how?

References

Cabinet Office (1991) *The Citizen's Charter*, Cmnd. 1599, HMSO, London.

Department of Health (1989) *Working for Patients*, Cmnd. 555, HMSO, London.

Department of Health (1992) *The Health of the Nation*, Cmnd. 1986, HMSO, London.

Department of Health and Social Security (1983) *The NHS Management Inquiry* (The Griffiths Report), DHSS, London.

Eddison, T. (1973) *Local Government: management and corporate planning*, Leonard Hill, Aylesbury.

Palfrey, C., Phillips, C., Thomas, P. and Edwards, D. (1992) *Policy Evaluation in the Public Sector: approaches and methods*, Avebury, Aldershot.

Glendinning, J. W. and Bullock, R. E. H. (1973) *Management by Objectives in Local Government*, Charles Knight, London.

Report of the Royal Commission on the NHS (1979) (The Merrison Report), HMSO, London.

Schulz, R. and Johnson, A. (1990) *Management of Hospitals and Health Services: strategic issues and performance*, C. V. Mosby, St. Louis.

Sheaff, R. (1991) *Marketing for Health Services*, Open University Press, Milton Keynes.

Welsh Office NHS Directorate (1992) *Protocol for Investment in Health Gain: respiratory diseases*, Welsh Health Planning Forum.

World Health Organisation (1985) *Health for All*, WHO, Geneva.

4

Evaluating Efficiency

What is efficiency?

The term 'efficiency' is often misunderstood and confused with the term 'economy'. Whereas economy is concerned with the costs involved in providing services, efficiency deals with the relationship between the inputs (costs) on the one hand and the outputs and/or outcomes (benefits) of services on the other. Efficiency seeks to assess what resources are used in providing services and what the services actually produce; in short it is the ratio of total benefits to total costs. Therefore, whilst financial costs are taken into account efficiency goes beyond a purely financial appraisal of a scheme to include broader issues, such as the inputs of care provided by family and friends in caring for people in the community or the effects of treatment on quality of life. What appears to be the most economical treatment is not necessarily the most efficient. For example, a scheme designed to discharge long-term patients from a psychiatric hospital due to close, to the cheapest alternative, such as health authority houses on a large housing estate in an area of relatively high deprivation, may well result in many additional costs being incurred both by the authorities and by society as a whole.

Why is efficiency important?

The level of funding of health and social care has aroused considerable debate in recent years, and the debate is likely to continue. Irrespective of the amount of money made available, choices will always have to be made as to where to spend it, how much to spend in each area and so on. It is exactly the same problem that confronts us all as individuals – how to allocate limited resources amongst unlimited wants and demands. In making such choices, individuals and organisations endeavour to generate the best possible outcomes or the greatest amount of output from their expenditure. Thus, in allocating funds to the provision of health and social care the aim of efficiency is to achieve the maximum output and the most favoured outcomes for society. The rationale for using efficiency as one of the criteria in evaluating health and social care is therefore to assess the validity of spending money on one scheme rather than others. For example, if a health authority is contemplating spending money on providing accommodation for parents of sick children it has to decide whether the benefits gained will be greater than if that money were spent elsewhere. The reason for this is that each pound spent on one service is one pound less available for another service.

How to assess efficiency

In order to consider the efficiency of any aspect of health and social care there are a number of distinct phases:

1. The description of the policy under which the project is being considered, alternative ways of achieving the policy goals, and the specification of the objectives for each of the alternatives.
2. The identification of all relevant costs and benefits associated with the project.
3. The measurement and valuation of the relevant costs and benefits.
4. The comparison between the costs and benefits, having adjusted for the effects of time and uncertainty and the choice of discount rate to employ.

5 The decision criteria with which to identify the most 'efficient' alternative.
6 The carrying out of a sensitivity analysis on the findings.

However, the nature of the benefits arising from health and social care may well differ considerably from programme to programme. Thus, the technique for evaluating the efficiency of a programme must reflect the nature of the programme's outcomes and their measurement and valuation in order that they may be compared with the costs of the programme.

We can now summarise the range of techniques available for evaluating efficiency (based on Drummond *et al.*, 1987; Palfrey *et al.*, 1992).

Techniques for evaluating efficiency

1 Cost minimisation
Where the outcomes of two policies are identical, or vary only slightly, and there is no significant difference in the effectiveness, then the choice between policies in terms of efficiency would be made on the basis of costs, with the less costly alternative being the preferred choice.

2 Cost effectiveness
In the large majority of case there will probably be differing degrees of success in achieving outcomes as well as differences in costs. The choice is then made on the basis of *cost per unit of effect*, or *effects per unit of cost*, with the policy with the least cost per unit of effect (or greatest effects per unit of cost) being the most efficient.

3 Cost–benefit
In most instances it is unlikely that the outcomes of policies will be identical. Indeed, comparison may need to be made between two completely diverse policies where the outcomes are entirely different. In order to assess the relative efficiency the outcomes would have to

be translated into a common denominator, usually a monetary measure, and the results stated in either the form of a ratio of costs and benefits, expressed in money terms, or as a sum representing the net benefit (or loss) of one programme over another.

4 Cost utility

An alternative measure of value to that of a monetary approach is one of utility. This sort of analysis considers the impact of the policy upon an individual's and society's welfare, expressed in some quantitative measure. This approach is being increasingly used in the evaluation of health care policies where *quality of life* adjustments are made to a given state of outcomes, whilst simultaneously providing a common denominator for comparison of costs and outcomes in different health-care programmes. The common denominator, usually expressed as *healthy days* or *quality adjusted life - years* is arrived at by adjusting the duration of the outcome (e.g. life expectancy) by the utility value of the resulting health status.

Each of the six phases outlined on p. 83 will now be considered and suggestions made as to how to undertake each stage.

Phase 1 – Description of the policy, alternative modes of implementation and specification of objectives

Although this initial stage may seem almost too obvious to be worthy of any discussion, until it has been undertaken adequately the subsequent stages have no foundation. The programme must be clearly described and the alternative ways of implementing it considered in order for the evaluator to have a reasonably clear perspective with which to construct the investigation. For example, a government policy designed to reduce the incidence of heart disease nationally could be tackled in a number of possible ways:

- Central government could intervene directly and levy additional taxation on smoking.
- Central government could provide extra resources to the Department of Health and Health Education Authority to undertake a series of health promotion programmes.
- Health authorities could be funded to employ additional health education officers, who could then implement local strategies to reduce the scale of the problem.

In this situation the evaluator would have to be aware of the policy aim (the reduction of heart disease), the alternative programmes (as identified above) and the objectives of each of the programmes. In deciding upon which technique to use the evaluator needs to be aware of:

- whether there is a fixed benefit or effect to be achieved (e.g. reduction in smoking prevalence by x%), and hence use *cost–effectiveness analysis*
- whether the objective is to increase *quality adjusted life-years* and use *cost–utility analysis*; or
- whether the objective is to ensure that the net social gain in monetary terms (e.g. the impact on gross national product of a decline in premature deaths and absenteeism associated with heart disease as compared with the costs of implementing the policy) is maximised and hence use *cost–benefit analysis*.

Phase 2 – The identification of all relevant costs and benefits

The use of economic evaluation within health and social care settings requires that *all* costs and benefits are identified: financial and non-financial costs and all outputs and outcomes need to be included.

Even though it may not be possible to measure and value all costs and benefits, all relevant costs and benefits associated with the programme need to be identified so that the decision-maker is fully aware of *all* of the consequences of the actions undertaken. As we have argued elsewhere (Palfrey *et al.*, 1992) the difficulties of quantification and valuation should not preclude the existence of all costs and benefits from the 'balance-sheet' of costs and benefits to be considered by the decision-maker. For example, as indicated in Chapter 1, in an attempt to identify and 'measure' the output (though not necessarily the outcomes) of the public sector, increasing use has been made of performance indicators. Batteries of these indicators are now being produced for the NHS, government departments, nationalised industries, local authorities and universities, among others. Performance indicators are a method of analysing statistical and financial data to gauge the relationship between inputs and outputs of the department or organisation, but should be used with caution since by definition they are 'indicators' of output and give no consideration whatsoever to outcomes.

Whether or not all costs and benefits are identified, the results of any evaluation should be subjected to a sensitivity analysis, where those costs and benefits which have not been measured and/or valued should be re-introduced in order to examine the reliability and accuracy of the findings. For example, if a project demonstrates a small net loss overall *but* only one or two of a long list of benefits have been measured and valued there is scope for speculation that if more of the benefits had been included in the calculations then the project might have shown a net overall gain. Further attention will be given to the use of sensitivity analysis under phase 6 below.

Phase 3 – The measurement and valuation of costs and benefits

1. *Costs*

When measuring the costs of a policy there are a number of issues which need to be addressed.

Firstly, it must be remembered that resources utilised in one area cannot be used in another. This notion of *opportunity cost* can be defined as the satisfaction gained from undertaking the next best alternative activity on a preference listing. Thus the total cost of a programme is the sum of benefits that would have been derived if the resources had been used elsewhere. In many cases the price that a person pays for a good reflects its opportunity cost and the pragmatic approach to costing is to take the existing market price wherever possible.

In situations where market prices are not appropriate (because, for example, they fail to consider the effects of the programme on third parties, known as externalities) or where they are not available, the evaluator may adopt the concept of *shadow prices*. For example, in terms of public health, clean air may be valued by the premium people are prepared to pay for houses in a 'clean-air zone'.

Secondly, another important concept is that of 'marginal analysis', in particular *marginal cost*. The marginal cost is the cost associated with one additional unit of product, activity or service. It is extremely important in the context of evaluation, because in many cases the alternatives will not necessarily be whether a particular service is to be provided or not, but whether the size of a service should be expanded or reduced. In such cases, the costs measured should be the cost of increasing (or reducing) the service, i.e. the marginal cost. For example, the cost of accommodating an elderly person in an under-utilised day centre is negligible whereas the cost of accommodating the same person if no space were available in existing centres within the community would be extremely high. Problems arise in evaluation when average, rather than marginal, costs are used since they fail to allow for variations in intensity of current resource utilisation.

The third aspect of cost measurement and valuation that needs to be carefully considered is the treatment of *capital costs*. These costs are incurred when the major assets, for example, the buildings and the equipment of the programme are acquired. Capital costs are not merely the sum actually paid for their acquisition and the interest payments on any loans used to fund such purchases. Account also has to be taken of the opportunity cost of using such assets in one particular way, thereby preventing them from being used elsewhere.

For example, long after the land, buildings and equipment have been paid for, there is a capital cost of continuing to use a hospital to provide health interventions, that is as long as it could be used in an alternative way. If the hospital could be sold, the opportunity cost would be its market value.

Another component which must be taken into account is the cost of using such assets, that is the depreciation of their value. Buildings and equipment do not last for ever, they have to be replaced and new ones paid for. By writing assets off over a period of time, using one of the methods of depreciation, a 'pool of funds' is then available to undertake the replacement. (For methods of how to calculate the allowance for depreciation see, for example, Horngren, 1972; Jones and Pendlebury, 1988.)

The White Paper *Working for Patients* (Department of Health 1989) proposed a new system of charging for capital in the NHS, with the aims of increasing awareness amongst health service managers of the costs of capital and using capital efficiently. *Capital charges* consist of elements for depreciation and interest and will be included alongside revenue costs in pricing health care services.

Fourthly, difficulties arise in the area of costs which are not unique to the project in question. For example, a hospital in-patient receives treatment which involves inputs of medical staff, other staff, drugs, dressings, diagnostic tests, etc. but the hospital also incurs other costs in the form of maintenance of grounds and equipment, general management, cleaning and so on, which are reflected in the overall costs of the hospital. However, if the system of marginal costs and marginal benefits is adhered to the evaluation need only consider the additional resources required to treat the patient, or alternatively, what resources may be released for the use of others.

2. *Benefits*

The measurement and valuation of benefits can be an involved and complicated process. Generally speaking the measurement of benefits revolves around the concept of *willingness to pay*, aggregated across individuals. In part the price that a person is prepared to pay reflects their willingness to pay although it must be remembered that the price that an individual is prepared to pay for an outcome may be constrained by income. Conversely the price that individuals actually pay for an outcome may understate their willingness to pay. For more details on this approach see Palfrey *et al.* (1992).

Methods of arriving at indicators of willingness to pay can be arrived at by asking people directly through, for example, questionnaires or by observation, e.g. the price people are prepared to pay for receiving treatment in a private hospital and avoid having to join a waiting list.

There are also other methods for valuing benefits which deserve some consideration. Where market valuations do actually exist, and they are not inflated by taxation, or understated because of subsidies, they should be used, subject to the conditions mentioned above. Other methods rely on estimates made by practitioners, professionals and policy-makers, e.g. the compensation paid by a court to offset the consequences of medical negligence could be used in the valuation process.

It has to be recognised that the valuation of benefits is often subjective and therefore it may not be appropriate to try and place a value on all identified benefits. In measuring benefits there are a number of problems, especially in trying to measure intangibles. Some progress has been made in the measurement of outputs and outcomes, most notably in the field of health (see Teeling-Smith, 1988), where there is now an abundance of literature on measures relating to quality of life. In addition, proxy and composite measures are used for measurement purposes. For example, mortality rates are often used as indicators of morbidity and the 'Jarman index' (1983) is often used to measure deprivation when resource allocation decisions are being made.

What is essential is that even if benefits (and costs) are not valued, or even measured, they must be, at the very least, included in the 'cost–benefit' balance sheet so that the decision-makers are fully aware of the consequences of implementing a particular programme. Benefits and costs not actually quantified and valued can then be 'allowed for' in the sensitivity analysis.

Phase 4 – Adjustments for timing and uncertainty

Most people would prefer to have money now rather than have to wait for it: they prefer current consumption to *potential* future consumption. Thus those costs and benefits which occur at the present time must be valued more highly than those which accrue in the future. In order to allow for this, future costs and benefits are *discounted*, to reflect what future money is actually worth now.

Thus if in six years time a project yields a benefit of £15,000, the present value is £11,193 (assuming a discount rate of 5%). This present value is arrived at by multiplying the amount of benefit (£15,000) by a discount factor, 0.7462 (which is in effect the value now of £1 in six years time). The choice of discount rate is in a sense arbitrary but in practice most projects using public funds adopt the *official test discount rate*, as recommended by the Treasury. In order to illustrate the concept consider a programme designed to rationalise the visiting schedules of home care assistants. If the programme yielded savings of £15,000 annually the calculation for the present value of all benefits at a discount rate of 5% would be as in Table 4.1.

Table 4.1 Present value of benefits

Year	Benefit	Discount factor	PV of benefit
1	15,000	0.9524	14,286
2	15,000	0.9070	13,605
3	15,000	0.8638	12,957
4	15,000	0.8227	12,341
5	15,000	0.7835	11,753
6	15,000	0.7462	11,193
		PV of benefits over six years =	76,135

This figure of £76,135 represents the value at the present time of £15,000 savings for each of the next six years, the non-discounted total of which would be £90,000.

One of the major reasons why people prefer current rather than future consumption is the fact that we live in a world of uncertainty – very little is guaranteed. Therefore, it cannot safely be assumed that the programme will definitely result in certain outputs and outcomes. The use of sensitivity analysis (see phase 6) is the usual approach to adopt in allowing for uncertainty.

Phase 5 – Decision criteria

There are a number of potential methods for assessing the worth of a range of alternatives, which we have summarised in more detail elsewhere (Palfrey *et al.*, 1992).

1. *Cut-off period*

A suitable period is chosen over which the costs incurred must be fully recouped. This may be because of the considerable uncertainty surrounding the benefits occurring in the future. However, the danger of such a method is that projects whose benefits do not materialise to any great extent until some time in the future would be disregarded. For example, the outcomes associated with a health promotion programme may not accrue for ten to twenty years. Despite the fact that such benefits are likely to offset the costs incurred many times over eventually, the project would fail to be allocated resources if the cut-off period method were employed on the basis of a ten-year cut-off period because most of the benefits would not become apparent until after that time.

2. *Pay-back period*

Instead of choosing an arbitrary cut-off period, the alternatives may be ranked according to the number of years necessary to recoup the initial outlay. It may be that in conditions of extreme political uncertainty, where safety is one of the over-riding considerations, such an approach may be appropriate. However, this method suffers from the same limitations as the cut-off period and should only be used alongside one of the more reputable methods, that is *Net Present Value* and *Internal Rate of Return*.

3. *Average rate of return*

This method simply aggregates the benefits associated with the project, divides the sum by the number of years over which the benefits accrue and expresses the result as a percentage of the initial outlay. However, on this basis a project which has a return of £1,000 in the first year and nothing thereafter would have a greater rate of return than one (with the same initial outlay) which achieved returns of £500 per year for six years. Another difficulty with this method is that no account is taken of the profile of benefits, that is a project which has benefits of £100, £200, £300, £400 in years 1 to 4 would have exactly the same rate of return as a project with benefits of £400, £300, £200 and £100 in years 1 to 4. In other words the effect of time on the value of future benefits is not considered at all in the method. This problem is rectified by using one of the more reputable methods, to which attention is now turned.

4. *Net Present Value (NPV)*

The concept of time preference was introduced in phase 4 above, where the technique of discounting was used to arrive at the present value of benefits and costs accruing in the future. The NPV of a project is thus the sum of the discounted benefits accruing during the project's lifetime less the present value of costs.

In deciding between alternatives the NPV approach would be to select the project with the greatest NPV, subject to a sensitivity analysis which adjusts for any uncertainties involved.

5. *The Internal Rate of Return (IRR)*

The IRR is another method which takes account of the effects of time. The IRR is basically the discount rate which equates the present value of all the benefits with the present value of all the costs, that is the IRR is the discount rate for which the

NPV is equal to zero. The IRR approach in deciding between alternative projects would be to select the project with the highest IRR.

Phase 6 – Sensitivity analysis

Economic evaluation is far from being a precise science and such evaluations need to be made with considerable caution. In undertaking an economic evaluation of a public policy it is therefore necessary for a sensitivity analysis to be incorporated. As the term implies, the approach is to test how sensitive the results obtained are by considering 'what if' type scenarios and questions. For example,

- What costs and benefits have not been included?
- What if costs increase by x%?
- What if benefits fall by y%?
- What if the discount rate is different?

In other words the effects of potential changes in the costs incurred, the benefits accruing from the projects and the discount rate will all have to be examined and the implications of such changes assessed before the results of the evaluation can be delivered to the relevant decision-maker(s).

Example: medical records

The need for an improvement in medical records has been well documented in health policy statements at national, regional, district and unit level. The Talbot Unit of Heartshire Health Authority is considering the appointment of an expert in medical coding and recording to achieve a maximum error rate of 1% in the coding of diagnosis and the recording of other patient information. The current error rate as indicated by Hospital Activity Analysis returns is in the region of

10–12% of all medical records. The unit has also committed capital money to the development of computer systems to accompany the initiative. However, there is considerable opposition to the initiative from a number of consultants within the unit who argue that the money should be spent on direct patient care.

How could the efficiency of the medical records initiative be assessed?

The following approach is based on the six phases discussed above.

Phase 1 – Description of the policy, alternative modes of implementation and specification of objectives

This has been more or less determined by the unit who need to justify their case that the medical records initiative is more efficient than the alternative of placing the funds into direct patient care. (In a real situation it would be advisable to seek to get a more explicit alternative than 'spending the money on direct patient care' although Chapter 3 indicated that objectives are commonly specified in vague and general terms.)

Phase 2 – Identification of all relevant costs and benefits

Costs

- Salary of project leader
- Training programme for medical records staff
- Delays, etc. incurred as a result of training taking place
- Changes in current procedures for dealing with medical records.

Benefits

- Reduced risk of inappropriate treatment being administered
- Reduced risk of litigation
- Time savings arising from not having to check incomplete or inaccurate records
- Improvements in communication between staff

- Improvements in communication between staff and managers
- Improvements in communication between hospitals and GPs
- Improvements in information for planning, resource allocation, performance review, quality assurance, contracting, budgeting, etc.
- Enhanced status of medical records staff
- Medical audit.

Phase 3 – Measurement and valuation of costs and benefits

Costs	*Measurement and valuation*
Salary of project leader	Annual salary plus additional costs
Training programme for medical records staff	Cost of training programme
Delays, etc. incurred as a result of training taking place	Additional time for records to be delivered – multiplied by hourly rate of medical records personnel
Changes in current procedures for dealing with medical records	Stress measurement techniques, rate of sickness absence, etc. – cost of replacement staff (?)
Benefits	
Reduced risk of inappropriate treatment being administered	Comparison of inappropriate treatments currently with estimate of proportion after initiative–difference multiplied by cost of time, drugs, etc.
Reduced risk of litigation	Comparison of litigation before initiative with estimate of number after initiative – difference multiplied by average cost of litigation to health authority
Time savings arising from not having to check incomplete or inaccurate records	Reduction in time to locate, check and deliver records – multiplied by hourly rate of medical records personnel

Improvements in communication between staff	Reduction in stress and conflict, reduction in sickness, reduction in cost of employing replacement staff
Improvements in communication between staff and managers	
Improvements in communication between hospitals and GPs	
Improvements in information for planning, resource allocation, performance review, quality assurance, contracting, budgeting, etc.	
Enhanced status of medical records staff	
Medical audit	

(Note that not *all* of the benefits have been measured and valued but they have been drawn to the attention of managers as being possible outcomes arising from the programme.)

Phase 4 – Adjusting for timing and uncertainty (using a discount rate of 5%)

	Year	£	discount	£	£
Costs of initiative					30,000
Benefits:					
	1	5,850	0.9524	5,572	
	2	11,200	0.9070	10,158	
	3	10,500	0.8638	9,070	
	4	7,350	0.8227	6,047	
Present value of benefits over four years					30,847

Phase 5 – Decision criteria

- If the cut-off period for recovery of costs incurred is *less than four years* then the initiative is not worthwhile, because it is not until during Year 4 that the project's benefits reach £30,000
- The initiative has a pay-back period of *just under four years*, that is all of the costs incurred could be repaid during Year 4
- The NPV of the initiative is: £

	Present value of benefits	–	30,847
less	Present value of costs	–	30,000

which results in a positive NPV of £847

- The IRR of the initiative is the discount rate which results in the present value of the benefits being equal to £30,000.

At 5% discount rate the NPV is equal to +847
At 6% discount rate the NPV is equal to +126
At 7% discount rate the NPV is equal to −582

At 6.2% discount rate the NPV is equal to 0

Phase 6 – Sensitivity analysis

	£
Estimate of costs not valued	0
Estimate of benefits not measured and valued	12,000
Present value of benefits if discount rate equal to 6%	+126

	%
Amount by which costs can increase	2.8
Amount by which benefits can fall	2.7
Internal Rate of Return to make NPV equal 0	6.2

Obviously this illustration is incomplete in the sense that not all of the benefits have been measured and valued. However, they have been estimated and included in the sensitivity analysis which provides an indication of the extent to which costs and benefits can change without affecting the net worth of the programme.

Difficulties in evaluating efficiency

The ideal scenario for evaluating efficiency would be where *all* of the costs and benefits associated with the programme could be identified, measured and valued. However, this is highly unlikely to occur and therefore judgements have to be made in relation to where to cut off the identification stage, how valid proxy valuations are, and so on. The choice of discount rate also causes much discussion in the literature although many evaluations have employed the 'Treasury test discount rate' as representing the opportunity cost of public sector investment.

However, many of the problems surrounding efficiency, especially in the field of health and social care, are associated with the outputs and outcomes produced by the services. Professionals argue that it is extremely difficult, if not impossible, to quantify and value care, the removal of pain, reductions in anxiety and so on and it is even less acceptable to place monetary values on these. However, the point has already been made that efficiency is not only concerned with money and the maximisation of a monetary output. Much recent work has concentrated on the production of Quality adjusted life-years (QALYs), for example, and the utilisation of cost utility analysis (see for example, Williams, 1985; Bryan *et al.*, 1991), which does not in any way discriminate between employed and unemployed, able-bodied and disabled, elderly and young, etc. As we have seen the objective of efficiency is to seek to obtain the maximum *benefit* for society from using the resources available, not the maximum financial gain.

Another concern that has been expressed is that efficiency takes no account of equity and equality, given the emphasis on achieving maximum output rather than on the distribution of the output. Attention will be focused on the evaluation of equity, equality and accessibility in Chapter 7, but it needs to be emphasised here that efficiency is only one of the criteria with which to evaluate any programme and it therefore contributes to the decision-making process rather than acting as the sole determinant of whether a programme should be implemented or not.

Summary and checklist

This chapter emphasises the need to be explicit in identifying all the costs, outputs and outcomes attributable to any programme. Wherever possible attempts should be made to measure these and place valuations upon them. The result of this process would be a 'balance-sheet' for decision-makers indicating the relative value of the programme in comparison with other programmes, where the resources could be utilised instead. The result would be that managers and professionals would have a clearer picture of how the resources available to them could be allocated in the most beneficial way.

It is worth concluding this chapter with a quote from one of the leading health economists, who has long argued that doctors and other professionals should be held responsible for the resources they commit to health care. Williams (1990) states:

> I even believe that being efficient is a *moral obligation*, not just a managerial convenience, for *not* to be efficient means imposing avoidable death and unnecessary suffering on people who might have benefited from the resources which are being used wastefully

The following checklist (adapted from Drummond *et al.*, 1987) should help managers and professionals to determine the relative efficiency of any programme they are contemplating.

1 Has the policy been specified in clear, precise terms?

2. Has a comprehensive description of the alternative(s) been provided (including the 'do-nothing' alternative)?
3. Have all of the important and relevant costs and consequences for each of the alternatives been identified?
4. Have the costs and benefits been measured in appropriate units (hours of working time saved, lost workdays, number of beds, etc.)?
5. Have the costs and benefits been valued credibly with the sources of such valuations clearly identified?
6. Have the assumptions on which valuations are based been made explicit?
7. Have the costs and benefits been adjusted for differential timing?
8. Has an incremental analysis of costs and benefits been performed?
9. Has a sensitivity analysis been undertaken?
10. Have the findings of the evaluation highlighted relevant issues to be considered by the policy-maker?

References

Bryan, S. *et al.* (1991) 'Chiropody and the QALY: A case study in assigning categories of disability and distress to patients,' *Health Policy*, 18, pp. 169–85.

Department of Health (1989) *Working for Patients*, Cmnd. 555, HMSO, London.

Drummond, M. F. *et al.* (1987) *Methods for the Economic Evaluation of Health Care Programmes*, Oxford University Press.

Horngren, C. T. (1972), *Cost Accounting: a managerial emphasis*, Englewood Cliffs, NJ Prentice-Hall.

Jarman, B. (1983), 'Identification of underprivileged areas', *British Medical Journal*, 28 (August), pp. 1705–9.

Jones, R. and Pendlebury, M. (1988), *Public Sector Accounting*, Pitman, London.

Palfrey, C. Phillips, C., Thomas, P. and Edwards, D. (1992) *Policy Evaluation in the Public Sector: approaches and methods*, Avebury, Aldershot.

Teeling-Smith, G. (ed.) (1988) *Measuring Health: a practical approach*, Wiley, London.

Williams, A. (1990) 'Ethics, clinical freedom and the doctors' role', in Culyer, A. J. *et al.*, *Competition in Health Care: Reforming the NHS*, Macmillan, Basingstoke.

Williams, A. (1985) 'Economics of coronary artery bypass grafting,' *British Medical Journal*, 291 (3) (August), pp. 326–29.

5

Evaluating Organisational Structures and Processess

What are organisational structures and processes?

In analysing an organisation people commonly examine both the organisation's *structures* – its roles and relationships – and its *processes* – the ways in which activities are carried out. 'Process' also refers to questions of motivation and leadership, interpersonal and intergroup relationships, power, organisational culture and managerial competences. These are the kinds of topics that one commonly finds as chapter headings in books on 'Organisational Behaviour', with different books showing variations in how the topics are grouped and related to each other and to other issues.

In practice, issues of structure and process are closely related; for example, the way in which managers undertake their work and the degree to which they are likely to delegate decision-making power to others (processes) will often be influenced by the span of control which exists within the organisation's structure.

In this chapter we will focus on those aspects of organisational structure and processes which we believe are the most useful from the point of view of evaluation. The emphasis is on highlighting approaches which can help managers, professionals and others to undertake an evaluation of how well an organisation (or a part of it) seems to be performing in its day to day operations. This differs from most of the other criteria in this book which concentrate more on the outputs and outcomes of the organisation's efforts.

Why are organisational structures and processes important?

Social care and health services are planned and provided by people working within organisations. In most cases, if an organisation's processes are not working well (for example, if there is more interpersonal hostility than cooperation) it is unlikely that the organisation's services will be delivered as effectively and efficiently as they could be.

Having healthy organisational processes does not guarantee that 'good' social care and health services will be provided, but sound processes come close to being a precondition for the effective, efficient and equitable provision of services which are likely to satisfy most of the target population for most of the time. Effective organisational processes are often a necessary but insufficient condition for 'satisfactory' services.

How to evaluate organisational structures and processes

Organisational structure

There are a number of ways in which an ineffective organisation structure can make the planning and delivery of high quality social care and health services unnecessarily difficult. One issue is that of *accountability and control.* The evaluator should ask whether clear answers can be given to the following questions: who is accountable to whom, for what and how? More formally, there should be agreement and clarity about the four dimensions of accountability (Elcock and Haywood, 1980):

- the location of accountability (*who*?)
- the direction of accountability (*to whom*?)
- the content of accountability (*for what*?)
- the mechanisms of control (*how*?).

There can be 'direct' and 'indirect' accountability. The former is the more obvious form in which individuals are accountable for their own work. Indirect accountability exists where managers are also held responsible for the work of their subordinates. In this situation the subordinates are accountable to their manager for their work (direct accountability) and the manager, in turn, is also accountable to his or her manager for the work of the subordinates (indirect accountability), as well as being directly accountable for his or her own work.

A second and related potential problem is *span of control.* This refers to the number of people that can be effectively managed by another manager. The span of control refers only to the number of people under one's direct control, that is at the next tier below the manager in question. For example, the span of control of a Director of Social Services can often be observed by counting the number of Assistant Directors – not the total number of staff working in the social services department.

If the span is too large (wide) managers will have difficulty in effectively monitoring the staff's progress, especially if the individual members of staff are working on complex and variable activities and are working at different locations. If on the other hand the span is too small (narrow), this can result in a lowering of morale because people feel their manager is 'interfering' too much in their day to day work – something that is more difficult for managers to do if they have a large span of control.

The issue is clearly related to the need for delegation. Generally speaking, the greater the span of control the more decision-making the manager will need to delegate in order to cope with the increased work-load of supervising the increased number of staff.

The span of control at the various levels within an organisation should be 'appropriate', neither too large nor too small. There is no magical number which is appropriate for all situations. The number of people who should be directly accountable to a manager is a matter for judgement in particular situations.

A third important issue is the *centralisation versus decentralisation* debate. There are tensions here between forces pulling in opposite directions. For example, centralisation of decision-making power is helpful if consistency in the provision of services is important. On the other hand, if responsiveness to local circumstances is the critical factor, decentralisation or delegation might be more appropriate.

If decisions concerning how services are to be provided are kept at the 'centre', individuals or units at the front line, providing services to clients, might feel that they do not have enough autonomy to be responsive to the needs of those for whom the services are intended. Some local authority social services departments have dispersed their staff to local area offices, but this does not necessarily mean that the control of budgets and other decisions have been decentralised. As various models of 'case management' emerge, decisions will need to be made about the extent to which budgets are delegated to particular managers.

A concept closely related to the centralisation versus decentralisation debate is that of *bureaucracy*. What is a bureaucracy? It is an organisation with the characteristics summarised below (Weber, 1947; Handy, 1985):

Characteristics of a bureaucracy

1 clear hierarchy of control, with authority flowing downwards and accountability upwards
2 prescribed roles possibly with job descriptions
3 specialisation and demarcation
4 rules and procedures (formalisation)
5 emphasis on vertical communications
6 expertise assumed to rest at the top of the hierarchy
7 promotion by merit selection and promotion are based on public criteria – e.g. qualifications, examinations, and proven competence – rather than on the unexplained preferences of superiors
8 impersonal rewards and sanctions (rewards, e.g. bonuses, and disciplinary sanctions are applied

impersonally and by standardised procedures, so that justice is seen to be done)

9 career tenure (job-holders are assured of a career structure and a job for life, in the expectation that they will commit themselves to the organisation).

This list of attributes describes the 'ideal model' of a bureaucracy ('ideal model' meaning the 'purest possible example', not the 'most desirable').

The benefits which can flow from a bureaucratic structure and its standardised procedures include:

(a) speed
(b) precision
(c) clarity
(d) continuity and predictability
(e) unity
(f) rationality and efficiency.

However, there are also a number of weaknesses or 'dysfunctions' in bureaucratic structures (March and Simon 1958; Ham and Hill, 1984; Child, 1977):

1 over-specific roles (employees have little opportunity to exercise discretion, and therefore do not feel 'involved'), and possibly low morale
2 a structure that is rigid rather than adaptable or responsive: change is difficult to achieve
3 rule/procedure drafters are unable to predict all situations; when unpredicted situations arise, staff have to decide how to deal with the case without being able to refer to a predetermined procedure.

In the case of some of the characteristics of a bureaucracy it is unclear whether they are helpful or damaging. For example, in 'service' organisations, such as local authorities and health care agencies, critics of 'rule bound' bureaucracies often advocate greater flexibility and discretion for the staff in dealing with the public. However, others (e.g. Hill, 1976) argue that such discretion tends to lead to:

- paternalism
- stigma
- personal prejudice; and
- uncertainty.

What is therefore needed is a system of 'rights' prescribed in well thought-out rules/procedures. Hill (1976, p. 81) argues that it is bad rules that need to be attacked, not rules as such.

Burns and Stalker's research (1961) suggests that while a 'mechanistic' structure (i.e. a bureaucracy) is appropriate for an organisation in a relatively stable environment, organisations which have to cope with a more unstable (changing/dynamic/fluid) environment need a more '*organic*' structure (what Handy, 1985, pp. 192–5, calls a 'task culture') one that is flexible, responsive, informal, and with continual re-definitions of people's roles.

Another structural option is the *matrix structure*, a system of project teams or task forces that cut across, or are 'superimposed' on, a number of specialist departments and taking members from each. Thus a particular employee might simultaneously be accountable to his or her line manager in the usual way and to a separate 'project' manager for certain aspects of the employee's work. The benefits of matrix structures are said to include:

(a) flexibility and responsiveness
(b) more open and potentially creative communication between different parts of the organisation

(c) a reduction in the decision-making load on senior management.

However, there are also potential problems with such structures:

(a) conflicting loyalties (role conflict, confusion, insecurity and anxiety)
(b) debilitating power struggles between the functional manager and the project manager
(c) people whose membership of project teams is temporary might wonder whether they will lose their place in the department's 'pecking order' while they are away; and they might experience 're-entry' problems when the project is complete.

The extent to which an organisation needs to be bureaucratic on the one hand or have a more flexible structure (e.g. an organic or a matrix structure) on the other depends on a number of variables, for example the organisation's size and the rate of change in the organisation's environment. As far as evaluation is concerned the task is to judge whether the structure of the organisation in question (or any particular part of the organisation) is *appropriate* for the circumstances in which it finds itself at any particular time.

Another key aspect of organisation structure to consider is an organisation's 'external' structure, that is the organisation's relationships with other agencies. A major feature of the reforms of the NHS and of local government in recent years is the division of organisations into *purchasers* and *providers* of services. An important task of those who wish to evaluate organisational processes in the reformed NHS and local authorities will be to inquire into the effectiveness of the new arrangements.

The new arrangements involve the introduction of elements of competition. These changes, it has been argued, will bring about improvements in the services being provided. In the

NHS, for example, hospitals (*providers* of health care) are now expected to compete with each other for patients. This can be done by persuading *purchasers* (such as health authorities and general practitioners) that they (the providers) can deliver high quality health care more cheaply than other hospitals. As far as organisation structures are concerned this means that there need to be managers within the system with clear responsibilities for defining and negotiating standards of care (for example, quality and service levels) and for measuring and controlling costs.

Similar 'purchaser/provider' splits have been developed in local government. Social services departments now have a duty to plan and organise packages of care for those in need of community care, but not necessarily to be the providers of that care.

These new arrangements imply new patterns of accountability. Instead of being directly accountable to line managers within a health or local authority, providers of service are more likely to be accountable solely through the enforcement of contracts or service level agreements, especially if the providers are in the private sector – an increasing likelihood with the further development of compulsory competitive tendering. This makes the task of the would-be evaluator more complicated in trying to disentangle the dimensions of accountability and control examined earlier in this section.

The changes also indicate a potential need for purchasers to undertake evaluations as 'brokers' to ensure that providers are delivering services that are effective in meeting the needs of the users.

Motivation and the design of work

Managers need to ensure that as far as possible staff can see clearly that increased effort on their part is leading to improved performance. Staff commonly enjoy a range of rewards when performance is high – 'intrinsic' rewards (like a sense of achievement and recognition) and sometimes 'extrinsic' rewards (for example, increased salary) if performance-related pay systems are in place. But if the efforts of staff do not lead to the improved performance which can bring about those rewards then it is unlikely that staff will be as motivated and committed to the job in hand.

There are three critical variables which influence the link between effort and performance, and an evaluator will need to inquire into the existence of these variables:

- *competence*: one needs to inquire into employees' competence to perform the work to the required standard; we will return to the issue of managerial competences later in this chapter
- *clarity of objectives*: staff need to know exactly what is expected and required of them; the setting of explicit objectives is an issue with which we deal in Chapter 3 on effectiveness
- *resources*: these include the necessary finance, equipment, material, information and time; if resources are inadequate then staff are likely to feel that performance does not depend solely on their efforts; frustration is likely to increase and levels of motivation fall.

An issue closely related to organisation structure and motivation concerns the kinds of jobs that people are expected to do. There are a number of approaches to designing (or re-designing) jobs, e.g. job rotation, job enlargement, job enrichment, autonomous work groups (socio-technical approaches), and 'core characteristic' theory.

From the point of view of evaluating organisational processes, the last mentioned approach offers the greatest promise, and it is the approach on which we will concentrate here.

The theory, developed by Hackman and Oldham (1980), and which we have summarised elsewhere (Palfrey *et al.*, 1992), suggests that there are five core characteristics which need to be built into a job if the job incumbents are to be highly motivated, if they are to enjoy job satisfaction and if they are to be effective – the principal desired outcomes of designing jobs. The five characteristics are indicated below.

Core characteristics for effective job design

(a) *Skill variety* – the extent to which a job entails different activities and involves a range of different skills and talents.
(b) *Task identity* – the extent to which a job involves completion of a whole piece of work with a visible outcome.
(c) *Task significance* – the extent to which a job has a meaningful impact on other people, either inside or outside the organisation.
(d) *Autonomy* – the extent to which a job provides freedom, independence and discretion in planning the work and determining how to undertake it.
(e) *Feedback* – the extent to which work activities result in direct and clear information on the effectiveness of job performance.

Hackman and Oldham suggest that, generally speaking, the more these characteristics are built into a job the more likely it is that the desired outcomes will occur.

The reason why this model is useful in the context of evaluating organisational processes is that Hackman and Oldham have provided a package to help evaluators:

- to decide how (if at all), and to what extent, a job needs to be designed; and
- to assess the extent to which the redesigning of a job has been a move in the right direction.

The package consists of:

- a questionnaire (a 'job diagnostic survey' on JDS) designed to be completed by the incumbents of a particular job

- a questionnaire (a 'job rating form'on JRF) designed to be completed by the manager(s) of those doing the job being analysed
- instructions for scoring the completed JDSs and JRFs
- a set of norms for evaluating the scores so that decisions can be made concerning the need for redesigning the job; the evaluation requires a comparison to be made between the averaged scores from the respondents and an appropriate set of norms expressed as means and standard deviations.

One of the weaknesses of the package for our purposes is that the norms are American and there is little or no information about the extent to which they are appropriate for other countries and cultures. There are, however, some norms which are specifically relevant to the health care management situation in the UK. For example, Eaton and Thomas (1991) collated the following norms for qualified clinical nurses in South Wales, one hundred of whom completed the JDS questionnaire (see Table 5.1).

Evaluators might wish to undertake a JDS – by asking a group of health/social care workers (minimum sample size of five) to complete the questionnaire provided by Hackman and Oldham – and to compare the results with the following (or

Table 5.1 Job Diagnostic Survey norms based on results from 100 qualified clinical nurses in South Wales

	Mean	Standard deviation
Skill variety	5.9	0.9
Task identity	3.7	1.1
Task significance	6.2	0.9
Autonomy	5.1	1.0
Feedback from the job	4.8	1.0

other) norms in order to assess how well the jobs in question are designed. If the mean score of a new sample of workers falls within one standard deviation of the norm for a given job characteristic, there is unlikely to be a need for the job to be re-designed. If the score is more than two standard deviations away from the norm (e.g. as a score of 4.0 for skill variety would be) then some improvement to the job's design is indicated, subject to certain other considerations spelled out in Hackman and Oldham's model.

Conflict

Differences of opinion about how services and policies should be planned, implemented and evaluated are extremely common. Such differences or conflicts are not necessarily damaging: they can often be positive and useful processes leading to creative ideas about how to deliver services.

On the other hand, conflict *can* be damaging, especially if it leads to staff spending as much time fighting 'political' battles as they do undertaking more productive work: much depends on how differences of view are handled. Examples of conflict which are likely to arise in the health and social care services include differences of opinion between:

(a) various departments within a local or health authority
(b) members and officers within a local or health authority
(c) members and other members (or officers and other officers) within a local or health authority
(d) one local (or health) authority and another
(e) professionals (e.g. medical practitioners, nurses or those in the professions allied to medicine) and managers
(f) managers in spending departments and managers in finance departments
(g) those responsible for providing health or social care services (for example, a Directly Managed Unit within a health authority) and those whose task it is

to represent the community interests (for example, a Community Health Council).

The causes of conflict

What *causes* conflicts within and between organisations? According to some researchers (e.g. Handy, 1985) the main causes are firstly objectives and ideologies, and secondly territory.

An example of the first kind of conflict could be the differences in priorities that sometimes occur between managers and professionals. Managers might need to control costs tightly at a time when health and social care professionals (such as medical practitioners or social workers) might feel that a higher priority is the improvement of standards of care.

The second type of conflict can arise when someone's 'territory' (for example, one's sphere of influence) is threatened or violated by some other member of staff. This kind of conflict is often evident in the practices of empire building, information control and interprofessional rivalry.

Evaluators will be interested in how effectively people within an organisation are dealing with conflict. Some organisations spend an inordinate amount of time dealing with problems of frustration, resentment and lack of cooperation; others deal with differences of opinion more productively through a combination of negotiated agreements, open communications and collaborative relationships. The latter approach is more likely to lead to the continued delivery of well planned services than the organisation riddled with interpersonal friction, intergroup hostility and closed information channels.

Team work

Some groups of staff work together more effectively than others, and evaluators need to be able to analyse 'what is going on' within groups or teams. There are several useful analytical frameworks available to assess the processes by which people work together in teams.

One approach to evaluating the effectiveness of teams – an approach to which we have previously drawn attention (Palfrey *et al.*, 1992) – is that proposed by Belbin (1981) who argued that the most effective teams are likely to be those in which a range of team roles are competently played out:

- *The chairman* – the stable leader who pulls team members together; able to find each member an appropriate role and acts as a unifier in the pursuit of common objectives; adept at drawing on the resources of the group, recognising where the team's strengths and weaknesses lie.
- *The shaper* – shapes the way in which team effort is applied; directing attention generally to the setting of objectives and priorities and seeking to impose some shape or pattern on group discussions and on the outcome of group activities.
- *The plant* – advances new ideas and strategies with special attention to major issues; looks for possible new approaches to the problems with which the group is confronted; is creative.
- *The monitor-evaluator* – high in critical reasoning ability; sound judgements not hindered by over-emotional issues.
- *The resource-investigator* – explores and reports on ideas, developments and resources outside the group; creates external contacts that might be useful to the team; conducts negotiations on the team's behalf; described sometimes as people who are hardly ever in the room, or if they are, they're on the phone!
- *The company worker* – works for the organisation rather than in pursuit of self-interest, and does so in a practical and realistic way; identifies with the organisation; has disciplined application and an orderly approach to work.

- *The team worker* – supports team members in their strengths (e.g. building on suggestions); underpins members in their shortcomings; improves communications between members and generally fosters team spirit.
- *The completer-finisher* – ensures that the team is protected as far as possible from mistakes of omission and commission, and actively searches for aspects of work which need a good deal of attention; maintains a sense of urgency within the team; high in self-control and self-discipline.

According to Belbin, people in groups generally fulfil two kinds of roles – functional roles (e.g. social worker, nursing officer, or general practitioner) and team roles (those outlined above). Belbin provides a questionnaire to help teams to see what roles are likely to be played in particular situations so that gaps can be identified. If, for example, there is no 'plant' in a group, fewer creative ideas will probably emerge than in a group which has a plant; if, on the other hand, there is no 'completer-finisher', the group is less likely to finish its tasks on time. Evaluating a team on this basis is a useful approach to team development.

With the increasing emphasis on interorganisational collaboration in health and social care (e.g. between local authorities, health authorities, voluntary bodies and the private sector) the need for effective team work has probably never been more important. The above approaches to assessing organisational "teams", therefore, has a role to play in evaluating organisational processes.

Group cohesiveness

An alternative approach is that advocated by Schein (1969) who suggests that group processes can usefully be assessed (possibly by the group members themselves with the help of a facilitator) by judging the processes in terms of:

- *Goals*: for example are the team's goals clear and agreed by all members?
- *Participation*: are all members involved and listened to?
- *Feelings*: are they expressed freely and honestly?
- *Diagnosis of group problems*: when problems arise are they carefully diagnosed so that the underlying causes can be dealt with?
- *Leadership*: do various members of the group provide leadership when appropriate?
- *Decisions*: are they made when necessary? is consensus sought?
- *Trust*: are communications between group members open and trusting?
- *Creativity and growth*: is the group flexible, innovative and developing?

When evaluating group processes in this way it is important to recognise that it is not a question of answering 'yes' or 'no' to the various questions but that each variable should be seen as a scale or dimension. It is a question of *the extent to which and the ways in which* the various processes take place.

The development of management competences

A model which provides a useful framework for the diagnosis and evaluation of managers' 'development needs' is the work by Pedler *et al.*, 1986 (see also Palfrey *et al.*, 1992). The 'qualities' of an effective manager are categorised below. A questionnaire is provided (in Pedler *et al.*) to help the evaluator to assess the strengths and weaknesses of a group of managers, and to plan what action needs to be taken to help the managers in question to develop their skills.

The characteristics of effective managers (Pedler *et al.*, 1986 are as follows:

(a) *Command of basic facts*: the level of awareness that managers have about their organisational plans, roles, relationships and networks.
(b) *Relevant professional understanding*: the technical or professional know-how which managers have about the goods or services being produced, the targeted markets, and the management principles which can help the organisation to perform effectively.
(c) *Continuing sensitivity to events*: perceptions of 'hard' information (e.g. statistics) and 'soft' information (e.g. political sensitivities within the organisation).
(d) *Analytical, problem-solving, decision/judgement-making skills*: not only the ability to respond rationally and logically in clear-cut circumstances requiring decisions to be made, but also the ability to make sensible judgements in uncertain and ambiguous situations.
(e) *Social skills and abilities*: degree of interpersonal skills, including those relating to communicating, negotiating, and persuading.
(f) *Emotional resilience*: the ability to cope successfully with stress when working to tight deadlines, and when dealing with uncertainty and ambiguity in situations where there is a good deal of interpersonal conflict.
(g) *Pro-activity* – inclination to respond purposefully to events: the ability to decide on, and achieve, goals on one's own initiative.
(h) *Creativity*: the ability to come up with new ways of dealing with situations, and to recognise and use the same ability in others.
(i) *Mental agility*: the ability to grasp complex problems quickly and the capacity to switch from one problem to another with some facility.
(j) *Balanced learning habits and skills*: the ability to think conceptually as well as in concrete terms.
(k) *Self-knowledge*: the knowledge that one has about oneself – one's values, goals, feelings, strengths and weaknesses.

An alternative approach is that developed by the Management Charter Initiative (MCI) in relation to the Accreditation of Prior Learning (APL) for managers (Simosko and Hall 1991). A framework is provided for the assessment (and if appropriate the accreditation) of managerial competences based on what is seen as the key purpose of management. The 'M1' standards specified for first line, or 'junior', managers see this key *purpose* in the following terms: 'To achieve the organisation's objectives and continuously improve its performance'.

The MCI framework identifies four key *roles* which managers need to fulfil in order to achieve the stated purpose:

- managing operations
- managing finance
- managing people
- managing information.

Each of these roles is then broken down into *units*, and each unit into elements. For example, 'managing operations' (the first key role) is broken down into the following two units:

- maintain and improve service and product operations
- contribute to the implementation of change in services, products and systems.

The first of these two units is then analysed into the following two *elements*:

- maintain operations to meet quality standards
- create and maintain the necessary conditons for productive work.

The hierarchical structure then continues so that each element is broken down into a number of *performance criteria*. When judging the extent to which a manager is achieving the necessary standards (by examining the available evidence against the performance criteria) regard should also be had for:

- *the range indicators*: that is, the various contexts in which one would expect the managers to be able to demonstrate their competences; and
- *the knowledge and understanding* which managers can be expected to possess in carrying out their work.

The framework is a thorough one (there are, for example, 163 performance criteria for the M1 standards) and assessment needs to be undertaken by a trained assessor to ensure that the evidence considered is valid, reliable, sufficient, authentic and current (Simosko, 1991).

Interorganisational collaboration

In the fields of health and social care services there is an increasing need for organisations to work effectively in collaboration with each other. Problems do not often fit neatly and exclusively into the remit of one organisation or another. An elderly person might have needs which can be addressed by statutory bodies (for example, health care agencies and social service departments), voluntary bodies and private sector agencies. An evaluation of -ganisational processes should therefore include an exam how effectively the interorganisational arrangeme

Such an evaluation may be undertaken b

- *Decision-making processes*: who h influence concerning the allocation assesses needs and to what extent

is planning undertaken by joint bodies? are participants rewarded for effective joint working?

- *Communication issues*: how effectively do the formal and informal arrangements work? do all the stakeholders feel that communications between the agencies are satisfactory? how effective are the information systems?
- *Resource management*: is each agency bearing its fair share of expenditure? how is such 'fairness' to be assessed and by whom?
- *Organisation development*: how are disagreements between agencies handled? how effectively are changes managed? to what extent are hidden agendas affecting progress?
- *Levels of collaboration*: is collaboration effective at strategic, operational and practitioner levels? and between professions as well as between agencies?

Case studies

To illustrate some organsational situations in which evaluation skills are needed in order to understand and deal with potential problems which might affect health and social care services, let us look at two case studies.

Example 1: IT – a case of change and conflict

In a social service department a senior team leader was told by her manager that a number of changes were going to affect her and her staff/colleagues in the near future. One of these changes involved the introduction of new ways of keeping records – using a new computer system.

The team leader knew from previous conversations with her staff/colleagues that several of them were, at [illegible]st, luke-warm about the idea of computerisation, but [illegible]as one change that she was extremely enthusiastic about. This enthusiasm stemmed from a visit to a neighbouring authority six months ago when the team leader became convinced of the advantages of the particular computer system in question which had been installed a year earlier – although not all of the staff in that authority agreed.

One of the department's staff (John Smith) in particular was a bit of an obstacle. He had worked for the authority for 30 years and was firmly opposed to modern notions of information technology (IT). He thought it dehumanised organisations and inevitably led to a poorer service for the department's clients (e.g. people blaming the computer when lapses in communications occur).

John Smith was in most respects an excellent performer. He was reliable, experienced, knowledgeable and, generally speaking, a sound decision-maker. He was also an influential leader within the department: many of the younger staff respected him and liked him. His one blind spot in the team leader's opinion was his attitude to IT, but the department could not afford to lose him.

The director of social services insisted that the new system had to be operating efficiently within three months.

How would you deal with this kind of situation?

There was clearly a good deal of conflict present here, with the potential for disruptive and counterproductive tactics. Some organisations deal with such conflicts more effectively than others. Organisations which can deal with the situation productively are those in which:

(a) there are open channels of communication between people so that they feel comfortable in confronting not only the substantive problem (the move towards computerisation) but also the process of change, including the disagreements and the ways they are being dealt with
(b) there is an appropriate leadership style so that, for example, John Smith can be given some influence

over the decisions which have to be made; there might be little choice about *whether* to computerise but there might be a good deal of flexibility about *how* it should be done; this might not be ideal from John Smith's point of view but it is preferable to him having no influence over events at all

(c) the managers involved have effective interpersonal communication skills.

One way to evaluate an organisation's processes, therefore, is to carry out an analysis of an organisation's communication channels, prevailing leadership style, and individual managers' interpersonal skills in dealing with a situation of this kind.

Example 2: Changes in the philosophy of nursing care

There is some evidence (Eaton and Thomas, 1991) to suggest that in nursing the dimension in Hackman and Oldham's model which is most likely to be absent is 'task identity' (the extent to which a job involves completion of a whole piece of work with a visible outcome). An approach to nursing which is now being implemented in an increasing range of nursing arenas is the idea of 'primary nursing'.

This approach to nursing is characterised by the following features (Macguire, 1989):

(a) Each patient is allocated to a named nurse, the primary nurse, who is responsible for and accountable to that patient for the whole period of his or her need for nursing care.
(b) The primary nurse has a 24 hour responsibility for the patient.
(c) The primary nurse is responsible for carrying out the nursing assessment of that patient, planning the nursing care to be given and evaluating the outcome of that care.
(d) Planning and evaluation of care is carried out in collaboration with medical staff and in conjunction with the patient and the patient's relatives.

(e) The primary nurse is responsible for co-ordinating the contribution of other health professionals to the care of the patient.
(f) A major part of the direct personal care given to that patient is given by the primary nurse.
(g) The primary nurse is assisted in the direct care of that patient by an associate nurse who takes over the giving of care when the primary nurse is not on duty. The associate nurse carries out the care as detailed in the care plan and must consult with the primary nurse before any major changes are made. A nurse may act in the capacity of associate nurse in relation to some patients and as primary nurse in relation to other patients.
(h) Each learner nurse is assigned to work with a named primary nurse and her patients.
(i) The primary nurse is supported in her work by a clinical specialist to whom she looks for advice in planning and evaluating care and for personal and professional guidance in her work.
(j) The primary nurse is supported by care assistants, clerical staff, and other non-nursing staff in the creation of a suitable environment for patient care.

Apart from benefits to patients, the use of primary nursing can bring benefits to nurses in terms of improved job design. This is because of the increased extent to which a primary nurse is likely to 'identify' with her patients and their needs, particularly because of points (a), (c), (e) and (f) in the above list.

The use of Hackman and Oldham's Job Diagnostic Survey can be used in 'before and after' evaluations of the implementation of primary nursing. This is likely to be an area for fruitful research in the future.

The difficulties of evaluating organisational structures and processes

Evaluating organisational processes has its problems. For one thing the criterion is a more subjective one than some of the others examined in this book. Sometimes, effectiveness and efficiency can be *measured.* Evaluating organisational processes relies more on *judgements* concerning the structure of organisations and the ways in which managers, professionals and support staff perform. But the subjective nature of the evaluation task does not mean that the evaluations will not be useful and important.

What is important is that organisational processes are evaluated as systematically as possible using frameworks and methods that are, as far as practicable, valid and reliable.

Summary and checklist

This chapter is far from being an exhaustive review of the available approaches to evaluating organisational structures and processes. There are many approaches which evaluators can choose from. What we have provided is a brief overview of the approaches to evaluating organisational processes which we believe can form an important part of the evaluator's tool kit.

The following checklist is offered as a useful framework for evaluating organisational structure and processes based on the ideas outlined in this chapter.

(a) Is the organisational structure appropriate and clear to all in the organisation?
(b) Are people's jobs well designed in relation to:

- Skill variety?
- Task identity?
- Task significance?
- Autonomy?
- Feedback?

(c) Are differences of opinion handled in ways which are productive from the points of view of all parties concerned?
(d) Do teams work well together?
(e) Do managers have the necessary competences to take the organisation forward effectively?
(f) To what extent do managerial processes (including planning, decision-making, communications, and control) help or hinder the achievement of the organisation's goals?
(g) Are the organisations which need to work effectively in collaboration with each other doing so consistently?

References

Belbin, R. M. (1981) *Management Teams*, Heinemann, London.

Burns, T. and Stalker, G. M. (1961) *The Management of Innovation*, Tavistock, London.

Child, J. (1977) *Organisation: a guide to problems and practice* Harper & Row, London.

Eaton, N. and Thomas, P. (1991) 'Primary nursing and job diagnostic surveys', *Paediatric Nursing* (July 1991), pp. 18–21.

Elcock, H. and Haywood, S. (1980) *The Buck Stops Where? Accountability and control in the NHS*, University of Hull.

Hackman, J. R. and Oldham, G. (1980) *Work Redesign*, Addison-Wesley, Reading, Mass.

Ham, C. and Hill, M. (1984) *The Policy Process in the Modern Capitalist State*, Wheatsheaf, Brighton.

Handy, C. (1985) *Understanding Organisations*, Penguin, Harmondsworth.

Hill, M. (1976) *The State, Administration and the Individual*, Fontana, Glasgow.

Macguire, J. (1989) 'An approach to evaluating the introduction of primary nursing in an acute medical unit for the elderly – 1: principles and practice', *International Journal of Nursing Studies*, 26 (3) pp. 243–51.

March, J. G. and Simon, H. A. (1958) *Organisations*, Wiley, New York.

Palfrey, C., Phillips, C., Thomas, P. and Edwards, D. (1992) *Policy Evaluation in the Public Sector*, Avebury, Aldershot.

Pedler, M., Burgoyne, J. and Boydell, T. (1986) *A Manager's Guide to Self-development*, McGraw-Hill, London.

Schein, E. (1969) *Process Consultation*, Addison-Wesley, Reading, Mass.

Simosko, S. (1991) *Accreditation of Prior Learning: a practical guide for professionals*, Kogan Page, London.

Simosko, S. and Hall, J. (1991) *Crediting Competence: a guide to APL for practising managers*, Management Charter Initiative, London.

Weber, M. (1947) *The Theory of Social and Economic Organisation*, The Free Press, Glencoe, Ill.

6

Consumers' Opinions and Service Evaluation

Who are the consumers?

Reference has been made in this book to service users, a term which includes all the people, not least informal carers, who are intended to benefit from health and social care services. The terms 'patients' and 'clients' are giving way to 'customers' and 'consumers' as health and social care policy recognises the move towards a mixed economy of care. In the new environment of separate purchasers and providers, the 'customer' could well refer to the purchasing agency rather than the intended beneficiary of care. This is even more probable since devolved budgets under the case management system of community care planning and provision are unlikely to be allocated to individual users. The 'consumer' is, therefore, a more appropriate term for the former 'client' and may be preferable to 'user' for two reasons:

1 The term 'user' has associations with drug abusers.
2 'Consumer', with its market-place connotations, seems a more accurate representation of the 'active citizen' model favoured by the present government.

We need, therefore, to consider the purpose of seeking consumers' opinions in the context of health and social care.

Why, they enquire of service providers, are you beginning to ask us what we think after all these years? What, in all honesty, is the answer going to be?

Phillipson (1991) lists a number of reasons why the 'notion of consumerism' has 'come on the agenda in the UK' regarding elderly people:

1 The emergence of a broader range of life-styles amongst older people.
2 The development of Charters of Rights – particularly in the field of residential care – has raised issues about the needs of older people as consumers of services.
3 The pressures facing informal carers.
4 The debate around the 1988 Griffiths Report and the Government's response in the White Paper *Caring for People* (Department of Health, 1989), together with the resulting legislation.
5 The debate about the political empowerment of older people and the need to combat the social creation of dependency in old age.

Unfortunately, these points focus only on secondary issues and beg the question of why, in the late 1980s, the pressures facing informal carers became recognised as a social phenomenon; why Charters of Rights began to appear; why the Griffiths Report of 1988 was commissioned and why the social creation of dependency – not only in old age but across all age bands of vulnerable people – became a debating point. All these 'reasons' quoted by Phillipson are manifestations of a consumerist approach to health and care policy rather than an explanation of why a consumerist approach has come to be so politically and professionally acceptable.

The Local Government Training Board (LGTB) in 1987 produced a document entitled *Getting Closer to the Public*, which urged public sector authorities to discover the public's views on a range of issues:

- Their preferences and priorities.
- The kind of services they want.
- Their knowledge of what services are available.
- Their views on the quality of service.
- The benefits that services bring them.
- Problems in how services are delivered.
- The image they have of the local authority.
- The things they would like to be done better/differently.

The LGTB booklet argues that by sounding out consumer opinions public sector staff will experience an improvement in morale through the knowledge that they are responding to the expressed voice of the public in future planning and provision of services.

Beresford and Croft (1990), in what purports to be a radical statement about consumerism as a philosophy of care, refer to the need for agencies to 'clarify what kind of involvement is on offer: information seeking, consultation or a direct say' and to 'make clear the limits of involvement'.

The implicit model of consumerism which emerges from much of the literature is that of a relatively powerless recipient of services whose views should be taken into consideration by those who have the authority to devise and implement policy. This is, indeed, the impression given by the government's White Papers, *Caring for People* and *Patients First*.

Why are consumers' opinions important?

Careful scrutiny of public statements about consumerism in the arenas of health and social care is important because it will enable us to frame appropriate questions. Chapter 2 referred to the need for honesty in designing formal or structured evaluation research. At the heart of any attempt to introduce a consumer perspective into organisational policy-making there should be an explicit definition by the organisation of what it understands by the term 'consumerism'. There is no point in asking members of the public whether they would prefer to attend a day centre or have a visit from a community nurse unless their preference is assured of influencing policy. In fact, this very question offers a limited option in terms of influence since it refers only to particular services available at a fairly lowly operational level.

Why the concept of consumerism has become a vogue idea in health and social care circles is that the government has decided that it should be so. The honest answer, therefore, to the question: 'Why are you suddenly asking us what we want?' is: 'Because we have been told to'. The government's policy of controlling public expenditure and encouraging a mixed economy of care has introduced a strong element of the enterprise culture into public service organisations. Commitment to the principle of public accountability – always the watchword of local government and the NHS – now has to be spelt out in health and social care plans. Central government policy demands greater 'choice' and 'independence' for service users. It follows a consumerist line. For care agencies to stretch the concept of consumerism towards the notion of 'empowerment' is to make demands that both the public and professionals are at present unwilling and unable to meet. The agenda remains securely in the hands of politicians, professionals and managers.

The consumer in the market-place

Why the term 'consumer' is an apt label for the developing social role of former 'patients' and 'clients' is that it entails only limited 'rights'. Members of the public have certain rights of redress for faulty goods or inadequate service; they have the right to discriminate between competing retailers and, most important of all, they have the right not to buy. Similar rights for care service consumers are beginning to take effect through complaints procedures and, occasionally, through the courts. But the right to discriminate between retailers of health and social care services and the right to refuse help are still constrained by professional attitudes and, in some areas, by law. The service user still has some way to go, therefore, before becoming a fully fledged consumer.

The consumer of commercial goods and services enjoys limited rights and very little power. While share-holders can participate in relatively confined areas of company decision-making, the general public have no direct way of influencing company policy or its organisational structure. Indirectly they can have some influence by 'voting with their feet' and avoiding particular retail outlets. A shrewd company will survive and grow by finding out what people think of their products. But no marketing research is likely to be asking questions to find out whether consumers would wish to have a greater say in how the company is run.

By accepting the soundness of the analogy of 'the consumer' in a mixed economy of care we are not necessarily arguing against any moral principle of user empowerment. We are stating what is and leaving aside any debate about what ought to be. In fact, the empowerment issue is being aired largely without any evidence of involving consumers and so perpetuates the very patronage which empowerment would abolish. By being pragmatic about consumerism as it might apply to health and social services, we can start to define those areas of planning and provision in which it is honest and potentially productive to seek people's views.

Consumers as survey planners

In Chapter 2 the point was made that the intended beneficiaries of health and social care services can contribute to the process of evaluation research design. Surveys designed to discover people's opinions about present and future services can benefit from asking them what they feel are their own areas of interest and concern. This exploratory groundwork is important because the responses can help to make the survey questions highly relevant to the consumer. The use of the word 'questions' here does not presuppose that the method of data collection will be the use of a questionnaire or interview schedule. It refers to the issues which are going to be central to the formal survey.

One of the most fruitful ways in which this preliminary information can be gathered is through group discussion. In marketing research parlance this would be called a 'focus group' interview. Clearly, the size of the group needs to be large enough to enable access to a range of views and yet not so large that the situation becomes formal or individuals are unable to make themselves heard. The representativeness of those taking part can be enhanced by holding a number of group discussions covering different localities, clinical specialties, ages or whatever variables are relevant to the survey's purpose. Some people feel more at ease in groups; others are more inclined to express their views in a one-to-one situation. There are more ways than one to clarify by preparatory work the areas of inquiry to be addressed in the substantive research programme.

Consumers as researchers

Chapter 2 discussed in brief the possible advantages in having lay-people as well as appropriately trained academics or staff taking on the role of researchers. There are examples in Britain of people with learning difficulties carrying out structured interviews as part of a consumer opinion survey not as volunteers but as paid research assistants. Policy statements expressing the need for collaborative approaches to health and social care planning (referred to in Chapter 2) concentrate on ways in which different professional groups and service agencies might usefully work together. The contribution that consumers could make as collaborative researchers is rarely discussed.

Consumers as participants

The main role of consumers in opinion surveys will be that of respondent or informant. The term 'respondent' refers to people who cooperate in the completion of a questionnaire whereas an 'informant' is sometimes used in the sense of 'interviewee'. 'Respondent' or 'participant' will be used interchangeably in the next few sections to mean anyone who is asked a question orally or in written form.

What are 'opinions'

There are a number of matters to consider before embarking upon a consumer opinion survey and these will be dealt with in turn:

- Aspects of evaluation appropriate to consumer participation.
- Access to participants.
- The representativeness of the sample of consumers.
- Methods of discovering opinions.
- Other considerations, e.g. data analysis.

Before turning our attention to these particular operational concerns, however, we need to clarify what we mean by 'opinions' and to classify them into certain categories.

Is there anything to be gained by trying to distinguish between, say, an attitude, an opinion and a belief? We cannot dwell on this issue here but would refer interested readers to the discussion in Palfrey *et al.* (1992), Sudman and Bradburn (1982) and Triandis (1971). For our purpose we can probably rely on common usage of these three words in order to find out whether they entail any conceptual difference.

Beliefs emanate from deeply held sets of values such as those expressed through religion or, for example, the American Constitution. Various concepts of citizenship, which are very relevant to issues in the field of health and social care, embrace fundamental principles of rights (of association, of freedom of speech, of liberty to travel, of religious commitment). Social science research has rarely attempted to discover this level of personal commitment. This is more likely to be a feature of studies in anthropology

Consider this question: 'Do you think the policy of community care is a good one?' What would a 'Yes' response tell us about the person who was asked that question? If no more probing questions were put, it would tell us only that the respondent held a favourable *opinion* or view in relation to the policy of community care. Why that opinion was expressed and how intensely it was held might never be discovered. We can not infer from the response that the survey participant holds a positive *attitude* towards the policy of community care. The reasoning behind the response could be:

> **I am neither in favour of community care nor against it. If anything, I think that residential care has a lot to offer. It all depends on the circumstances. Unfortunately, residential care has not been properly managed or staffed. As a result it offers poor quality care at present. So compared with residential care, community care is probably a more attractive option.**

An alternative attitude underlying the expressed opinion might be this:

> **Residential care is socially unnatural and as an option it allows many relatives to duck out of their moral responsibilities. Informal carers certainly should have outside support where necessary and this is what community care is all about.**

An *attitude* indicates a certain predisposition towards or away from general 'social objects' (Oppenheim, 1992), whereas an opinion applies to more specific, often contextual objects. It might be important for the purposes of evaluation to dig beneath the level of opinion in order to reach people's attitudes. Opinion polls often tell us no more than how part of the electorate is likely to vote. Just why they intend to vote that way – or why they choose not to vote at all – is a far more interesting and complex matter.

Although we shall use the term 'consumer opinions' to stand for consumer opinions *and* consumer attitudes it is important for anyone carrying out a formal evaluation to recognise the limitations of the data produced by questions framed to elicit relatively superficial responses. We shall return to this potential problem later in this chapter.

Types of opinions

We now turn in more detail to certain methodological issues raised in Chapter 2. When people are asked to cooperate in a piece of marketing research or a survey the chances are that they will agree, especially when they are asked face-to-face, although response rates from postal questionnaires often reach no more than a 40% level. Considering that survey or research participants are very rarely compensated for their time, either with gifts or money, we might reflect upon why they take the trouble to cooperate in such relatively high proportions. The possibility that only well motivated people respond to postal questionnaires raises questions about possibly unrepresentative data. The fact that projected samples of participants actually take part in a consumer survey can be very reassuring but it may also be deceptive. Just because people answer survey questions does not guarantee that their expressed opinions are of any research value. Three types of deceptive opinions are set out below:

1. *Uninformed opinions*

One consideration that is frequently ignored in the construction of survey questions is that people may be relatively ignorant about the topics covered in some of the questions and yet still provide responses. Unless uninformed opinions are recognised as such and discarded prior to the analysis stage of the survey the data which results from such uninformed responses may provide invalid evaluation data. It is probably a trait of human nature that, once put 'on the spot' after having agreed to take part in an interview or to complete a questionnaire in the presence of the researcher, people will avoid displaying ignorance. Uninformed opinions may arise out of:

- lack of information about the topic
- misinformation
- misinterpretation of the question
- lack of familiarity with certain words or phrases

Example: postal questionnaire

Let us assume that as part of a postal questionnaire to carers of relatives suffering from Alzheimer's Disease, the following question appeared:

> **'The implementation of the NHS and Community Care Act will bring benefits to carers.' Do you agree or disagree with this statement?**

Even if an 'agree' or 'disagree' box has been ticked, how can we tell that the response is to be taken seriously? The carer may not actually know what the Act lays down or may be under a misapprehension about its proposals. Is the carer's understanding of the word 'benefits' the same as that intended by the question-setter? Can we assume that 'implementation' is a word that is of sufficient currency to be part of the lay person's vocabulary?

In order to avoid assumptions about people's capacity to answer questions meaningfully it is important to think through the possibilities of receiving uninformed reponses. A pilot study should be carried out in which a number of people as similar as possible to those intended as the main sample are asked to comment on the draft questionnaire or interview schedule. Even before this stage is attempted, a collaborative effort between consumers and research supervisors could produce an outline of areas to be covered and possible questions to be tested during the pilot stage.

2. *Second-hand opinions*

Oppenheim (1992) has pointed out that opinions derived from what he calls 'attitudinal predispositions' are rarely the product of a balanced appraisal of all available evidence. As a rule, says Oppenheim, 'attitudes are acquired or modified by absorbing, or reacting to, the attitudes of other people'. Opinions, then, which derive mainly from other people's experience are hearsay. In courts of law evidence based on hearsay is inadmissible. The same should be true of opinion surveys.

In weeding out second-hand opinions, the same technique applies as in all instances where the validity of data generated by opinion surveys needs to come under scrutiny. Questions which precede or follow main questions allow for information to be gleaned about the respondent's knowledge or interpretation of a particular question. Without making an interview schedule or a questionnaire unduly long, certain checks can be built in which help in the data analysis stage. Relating back to the Alzheimer's Disease example above, preliminary questions could discover whether the participant had accurate and adequate knowledge of the Act. These 'filter questions' are usually followed by an 'If yes/no . . .' question construction.

Example (extract from questionnaire)

5(a) Have you heard of the NHS and Community Care Act?

Yes

No

- If you have answered 'no' please go to Question 6.
- If you have answered 'yes':

5(b) Could you write down in one or two sentences what you understand to be the main purpose of the Act.

5(c) What effect, if any, do you think that the Act is likely to have on the work done by family carers?

For further reading about the various ways in which cross-checks and secondary analysis can be incorporated into sets of survey questions in order to monitor the validity of responses, see Belson (1981).

One important consideration, of course, in compiling questionnaires is whether the kind of information being sought would be more accessible through the medium of an interview. One criterion which could help to solve this question is the developing structure of the draft questionnaire. If, for example, an intended postal questionnaire is becoming excessively lengthy and complicated, it may well be advisable to change the set of qusetions into a semi-structured interview. This will allow ambiguities of question wording to be resolved for the respondent and for probes to be made which help to verify whether there is a sound knowledge base on which responses can be made.

3. *Non-opinions*

We have noted above that consumers of health and care services may, during a survey, be happy to record an opinion during interview or on a questionnaire form even though they have little or no knowledge of the topic being explored. This tendency to give some response may arise out of a certain apprehension about being seen to be ignorant about an area of knowledge but it could also reflect a prejudiced position on certain issues. We have also drawn attention to second-hand opinion which, in some circumstances, might provide the only 'information' – or misinformation – on which to base an opinion. There is a third type of deceptive opinion. This is a non-opinion masquerading as an actual opinion.

Some interesting research has been carried out in order to test the extent to which the wording and context of survey questions affect the responses. Billiet (1991) has summarised the findings from a number of question wording experiments and has classified four types of 'response effect'. In connection with the issue of non-opinions appearing as bona fide opinions the most relevant example from the research is the result of 'question constraint'. This happens when the checklist of possible responses omits categories that many respondents would use if they were available. Billiet uses the following example to illustrate the point:

Question constraint

Using a filter question			*Not using a filter question*
Nowadays people talk a lot about the European Community. Do you feel that the fact that Belgium is a member of the EC is a good thing, a bad thing, neither a good nor a bad thing, or don't you have an opinion on that?			Nowadays people talk a lot about the European Community. Do you feel that the fact that Belgium is a member of the EC is a good thing, a bad thing, or neither a good nor a bad thing?
Responses	%	%	
A good thing	49.2	60.7	A good thing
A bad thing	1.7	2.1	A bad thing
Neither . . . nor	15.6	36.1	Neither . . . nor
No opinion	33.5	1.1	(No opinion)

Responses to one set of questions offering the category 'No opinion on that' and another set omitting this response option clearly indicate that people who really have no opinion will feel constrained by the limited number of options to record an opinion.

We now deal with those matters, highlighted earlier which need to be considered before planning a consumer opinion survey.

Which aspects of evaluation are appropriate to consumer participation?

Previous chapters have dealt with the *components* of a systems model as a framework for evaluating health and social care programmes and certain *criteria* which can be used as yardsticks for assessing various aspects of services. Of the components discussed in Chapter 1 those of greatest concern to consumers are likely to be *process* and *outcome* and the most relevant criterion that of *effectiveness*.

Process

Sometimes, in attempting to discover whether designated outputs improve the well-being of patients or social care recipients, the way in which those outputs are achieved may escape attention. The performance indicators referred to in Chapters 1 and 4 may all be highly commendable targets designed to enhance efficiency and sensitivity to public demand. But there is another dimension without which quality assurance remains only partially defined. To the question: 'What has been achieved?' must be added: 'And how was the process of achieving it regarded by the consumer?'

The amount of time that people have to wait in an out-patients' department may be reduced in accordance with a targeted average number of minutes. But this output may be achieved at the expense of courtesy and comfort. Efficiency could become regimentation. On the other hand, members of the public might prefer a highly efficient if rather impersonal means of gaining access to medical staff as opposed to a very personalised form of public relations which accompanied an intolerable waiting time. Without consulting people about how they feel about this aspect of health care we impose on them limited administrative or professional views about how to balance issues of process with those relating to output.

Similarly, in the context of social care, one output of a home care service may be measured according to the indicator of increased hours per client or a domiciliary service might meet a target of delivering meals on wheels to more elderly people in need of that service. Yet these 'interventions' may be appreciated more by consumers for the way in which the events break up the day and offer a chance to have some company. In other words, the quality and perceived benefit derived from the process of providing a service could be more important, for many people, than the service itself.

Outcome

The evaluation of outcome is usually approached by measuring the impact which a particular output has had on individual service consumers. The preceding section, however, illustrates the potential importance to the recipient of the way in which aspects of care services are 'delivered'.

The process of actions and interactions produces a series of outcomes which can be monitored by asking consumers about the extent to which the process has improved their sense of well-being, improved their levels of self-confidence or the extent to which any other agreed criteria are perceived to have been attained.

The effect of *outputs* upon a person's quality of life are also important to evaluate. The problem, however, with a number of programmes which are subjected to evaluation is the difficulty in correlating outcomes with specific outputs. For example, it would be all too easy to assume that the provision of security locks on all windows and doors would have the effect of making disabled persons feel safer within their own homes. In fact, it could have the effect of making that person feel more threatened. On the other hand, an increased sense of safety from harm after the installation of security locks might be entirely coincidental. Another factor might have produced the effect. For example, an adjacent property which was previously empty may recently have become occupied by a friendly, reassuring neighbour. A good deal of information about the possible cause–effect relationship between outputs and outcomes can only be gathered by asking consumers of health and social care services.

Effectiveness

This criterion relates to the previous point concerning the extent to which an objective has been unequivocally achieved by some process or output. The part which consumers can play in testing, for example, the effectiveness of services, treatments, care programmes, or physical facilities is not only at the formative or summative evaluation point but at the very outset, at a time when what will constitute 'effectiveness' is being defined.

St Leger and colleagues (1992) use the term 'efficacy' as one index of effectiveness in the field of health care. In clinical terms, a procedure may be said to be efficacious if it can be clearly demonstrated to have had a beneficial effect on prognosis or suffering. Findings from studies of efficacy are usually expressed as percentages of patients improving or in remission after specified periods of time, and the customary method of evaluating efficacy is the randomised controlled trial.

St Leger draws attention to the developing interest in health care evaluation studies in more qualitative data derived from interviews with patients and the analysis of case studies. Thus what constitutes 'good care' in the opinion of patients may not equate neatly with 'efficacy' as defined by medical practitioners.

How to gain access to consumers

Gaining access to consumers in order to canvass their views may be thought of as a three-part process:

- Gaining physical access
- Gaining acceptance
- Communicating.

Gaining physical access

This includes not only face to face interviews, either individually or in a group situation, but ensuring that questionnaires, for example, reach the intended sample participants. Telephone interviews are used much more frequently in marketing research than in social research but provided that the sampling procedure is random and, as with all data collection methods, the potential for sample bias has been carefully thought through, interview by telephone can afford immediate physical access to respondents.

Other methods of gaining access are:

- *street intercepts* – a device familiar to most of us when stopped in the centre of town by someone clutching a clip-board

- *door-knocking* – perhaps the most invasive approach; census enumerators adopt this method but they have legal authority to ensure public participation
- *visiting a gathering place* – such as a place of work, a community centre or a clinic
- *approaching a captive audience* – for example, a research nurse interviewing patients on a ward or interviews arranged with residents of a home.

These and other methods of 'getting to' prospective consumers need to be negotiated with sensitivity. Eager researchers might be prone to believe that everyone is as interested in and committed to the evaluation as they are when what they are asking people to do is to give up their time and share often very personal thoughts with a complete or comparative stranger.

Gaining access to large numbers of consumers can be difficult and time-consuming. Some of the methods mentioned above can be adopted depending on the nature of the evaluation and the sample sizes involved. There are times, however, when the evaluator will find that personal access is not feasible on the scale required and may have to rely on intermediaries – such as carers, colleagues, or voluntary organisations – to relay the data collection instrument to the intended participant and the data back to the evaluator. Losing some control over the evaluation process in this way with accompanying concerns about collusion and sample integrity may be the price that has to be paid for the retrieval of maximum data.

Gaining acceptance

Gaining access to people does not necessarily mean gaining access to their opinions or attitudes. A range of skills are needed in order to ensure that an interview will take place or that observation can be carried out. These skills can, perhaps, best be illustrated by listing the manoeuvres involved in negotiating what might be called a research or evaluation 'episode':

- Fully inform people about the purpose of the evaluation, its scope, the time involved for each person willing to take part and who will read the report(s)
- Assure them of confidentiality at all stages of the evaluation
- Be prepared to show proof of your identity and credentials
- Unless, for some reason, there is an embargo on the release of a report, offer to provide access to any written documents to all participants in the evaluation.

These simple precepts of research etiquette should ease the way towards gaining acceptance. Breaches of etiquette serve to impede not only one's own attempts to evaluate services but those of others coming after.

Communicating

Although aspects of communication have been included in the two previous sections on access and acceptance, it is worth highlighting as a separate issue. Access and acceptance will count for nothing if the verbal exchanges between evaluator and respondent are clouded by misinterpretation. Ridding a questionnaire or interview schedule of jargon and ambiguous words and phrases is a task to be achieved most economically by involving consumers in the first draft stage, i.e. as part of a pilot study. Mann (1968) is still a valuable guide through the minefield of inept question construction. Some of the data collection methods other than questionnaires and interviews are also heavily dependent for their successful application on clear communication. These are dealt with later in the chapter.

How can we be sure that our sample is representative?

The advantages of conducting a pilot study prior to engagement in the formal evaluation itself have already been mentioned. In determining who should constitute the pilot sample the need for random selection is not so crucial as it will be in the substantive evaluation research. The key consideration is to find a number of people whose attributes – e.g. age group, diagnosis and/or social care needs – closely resemble those of the intended main sample. In some situations compromises may have to be made but it would be unwise to depart too far from the 'profile' of the proposed main sample for reasons already stated in the previous section.

The inevitable question which arises when a survey sample is being considered is: 'How large should the sample be?' The question is capable of being answered in two ways. First of all, there is a case for saying that the selection of a sample size depends on a matter of judgement, but there is also a more statistically based answer.

Example: the 'population' on a ward

You wish to record and analyse the views of patients on Ward A about their first impressions on being admitted to the hospital. The total number of patients on the ward is 30. What constitutes an adequate sample size? Common sense tells you that a sample of 10, even randomly selected, can not guarantee that the aggregate of views expressed will be representative of the total number of patients on the ward. But at which point would you 'feel' that the right number had been reached? Probably the majority of researchers would consider fewer than 20 to be an inadequate sample size. Gaining the views of two-thirds of the total 'population' on the ward somehow gives a sense of acceptability – a sense of relative assurance that the results will validly represent the views of the missing one-third.

There are, however, statistically computed tables which indicate an adequate sample size from a given total population – adequate, that is to say, in its capacity to provide a set of data which can be taken as highly representative of the population as a whole. In the above example, the recommended sample size would be 28. Perusal of these statistical tables will show that as the total population rises the adequate sample size reduces in terms of its ratio to that total population. For example, whereas a 93% sample would be indicated for our ward survey, if three such wards were combined to make a total population of 90 patients, a sample size of only 81% would be adequate and if we were to extend the survey to every patient in the 1,000 bed hospital we would only need to ask the views of just under 28%. In essence, therefore, a system of 'diminishing returns' operates in establishing what an adequate sample size really means. That is why it may surprise many people that a sample of around 1,200 can be taken to represent the whole of the British population for the purposes of opinion polls.

The issue of reaching an acceptable sample is dealt with in numerous books on social research and survey designs. Fitz-Gibbon and Morris (1987), for example, provide comprehensive treatment of the various types of sampling procedures and their relevance to the process of evaluation. Decisions about sample size are closely linked to the selection of an appropriate evaluation research design. The statistical tables normally start at the number 10. Evaluation may, however, legitimately dip below this figure if a research design other than a survey type is to be used – for example a case study or life history.

How can we discover people's opinions?

In Chapter 2 reference was made to various methods of collecting qualitative data. These are: interviews, observation, scrutiny of relevant documents and questionnaires. All these methods can also be applied to the collection of quantitative data. For example, documents consulted might be entirely statistical and questionnaires might also be at least partly concerned with eliciting quantitative data.

In addition to the methodological tools outlined in Chapter 2 there are others which are available and which have their own particular strengths. The two outlined below offer additional or alternative means of probing both consumer opinions and attitudes.

The Delphi technique

The original oracle at Delphi in Greece was deemed capable of delivering utterances informed by divine inspiration. In the modern world of social research, the reference to Delphi has assumed a connotation that is more secular and somewhat more fallible. The 'oracle' in this context refers to a person who is considered to be an expert in a particular area of knowledge and/or practice. In the field of nursing, for example, the Delphi technique has been used in order to identify which particular areas of nursing were deemed to be of highest priority for research (Macmillan, 1989).

Essentially, the technique involves the development by the researcher of informed propositions derived from considerable secondary research – particularly by a thorough search of relevant literature and documentation – and from exploratory interviews with experts other than those who will ultimately form the panel. A questionnaire is then constructed and piloted with a further group of experts and the final product is sent to prospective panel members soliciting their views on specific topics. The responses are summarised and fed back to the respondents. This procedure may be repeated two or more times until the sets of responses fall into patterns of consensus.

Although this technique has considerable advantages in generating a core of agreed opinions about key aspects of organisational planning, the panel of experts almost always consists of professionally trained staff. The opinions of consumers have usually been given expression through the medium of structured interviews. Now that patients and clients are being seen as consumers by health and social care planners and providers, their areas of expert knowledge as service consumers can be harnessed by applying the Delphi technique in the collection of data. Such an approach would be particularly enlightening in an evaluation study which compared consumers' 'core' opinions with those of professionals.

Diaries

The relative superficiality of the qualitative data gained from the use of questionnaires and the more structured interviews can be offset, complemented or substituted by asking a sample of people to record their feelings about events centred on health and social well-being. The much more intimate comments that diaries often contain can be of great benefit in monitoring the impact of care provision on its recipients. Some studies in family health have used diaries to discover how family members develop specific ways of maintaining health and preventing illness (Boyle, 1985; Roghmann and Haggerty, 1972).

More use could be made of diaries in both health and social care evaluation. The obligation placed upon social services departments to assess individual needs and to ensure that services are provided or bought in to cater for those needs underlines the appropriateness of evaluating the care provided against the yardsticks of consumer expectations and actual experience. Diaries would give carers an opportunity to keep a record of their response to the ways in which care packages are having an impact on their quality of life and on the quality of life of those for whom they care.

Other considerations relevant to formal evaluation

There are other considerations which need to be taken into account before embarking upon a formal evaluation. Two of the most important are *ethical issues* which may have to be borne in mind where, for example, a research design entails the introduction of an innovative approach to care, with experimental and control groups. The other major concern will be to determine *how the data will be analysed.* Some aspects of data analysis are dealt with in Chapter 2. The works by Miles and Huberman (1984), Strauss (1987) and Silverman (1985) amongst others, offer extensive coverage of analytical techniques related to the various data collection methods.

Some potential problems in discovering opinions

We can highlight four of these:

- Compiling interview schedules and questionnaires which are capable of producing reliable and valid data is not an easy task. The tendency, however, may be to opt for one of these methods of data collection because they give the impression of being more 'tangible' than the more free-ranging interview or types of observation. The need to test out a set of proposed questions before engaging with the actual evaluation can not be over-emphasised.
- Overt participant observation – which may well involve identifying opinions and attitudes – is likely to take longer to gain acceptance from participants than most other means of collecting qualitative data. Establishing not just rapport but trust may not be achieved without a good deal of preparatory work with a prospective sample of consumers.
- Not all data needs to be subjected to statistical analysis. Although opinions, for example, can be classified into groups of responses which can then be expressed numerically – for example, in percentages, ratios, averages – this kind of analysis and presentation might not be necessary. The most sophisticated means of analysis cannot rescue an evaluation which has used flawed methods of data collection.
- One research instrument is likely to produce only partial data. Interpreting people's behaviour by means of observation could lead to inaccurate meanings being attached to that behaviour. In order to provide a more rounded and more valid interpretation, follow-up interviews could be used to advantage. This pluralistic approach to evaluation is one which we have previously advocated (Palfrey *et al.*, 1991, 1992).

Summary and checklist

This chapter emphasises the logic and the advantages of involving the intended beneficiaries of care services in all stages of evaluation. It also draws attention to the possibility of consumers actually carrying out evaluation data collection rather than playing their customary role as relatively passive survey 'respondents' and 'interviewees' (Whittaker, Gardner and Kershaw, 1991). As far as consumer opinions are concerned a number of points have been made:

- There are various types of opinions.
- Conventional data collection methods are often limited in their capacity to gauge intensity of opinions.
- Other methods of data collection are better suited to probe beneath opinions in order to probe attitudes and feelings.
- There are ways of trying to minimise the possibility of accepting opinions at face value when they might be based on inadequate, inaccurate or second-hand information.
- Efforts at seeking consumers' opinions are very worthwhile because the data produced helps to counteract exclusively professional perceptions of effectiveness.

References

Belson, W. A. (1981) *The Design and Understanding of Survey Questions*, Gower, Aldershot.

Beresford, P. and Croft, S. (1990) 'A sea-change', *Community care*, 834, pp. 30–1.

Billiet, J. B. (1991) 'Research on question wording effects in survey interviews', *Graduate Management Research*, 5, (4) pp. 66–80.

Boyle, J. S. (1985) 'Use of the family health calendar and interview schedules to study health and illness', in Leininger, M. N. (ed.) *Qualitative research methods in nursing*, Grune & Stratton, Orlando.

Department of Health (1989) *Caring for People*, HMSO, London.

Department of Health and Social Security (1983) *The NHS Management Inquiry* (The Griffiths Report), DHSS, London.

Dull, R. (1988) 'Delphi forecasting: market research method of the nineties', *Marketing News*, 22 (18) (August), pp. 17.

Fitz-Gibbon, C. T. and Morris, L. L. (1987) *How to Design a Program Evaluation*, Sage, Beverly Hills.

Jain, C. L. (1985) 'Delphi forecast with experts opinion', *Journal of Business Forecasting* 4 (4) (Winter), pp. 22–3.

Local Government Training Board (1987) *Getting Closer to the Public*, LGTB, Luton.

Macmillan M. S. *et al.* (1989) *A Delphi Survey of Priorities for Nursing Research in Scotland*, University of Edinburgh Department of Nursing Studies.

Mann, P. H. (1968) *Methods of Sociological Enquiry*, Blackwell, London.

Miles, M. B. and Huberman, A. M. (1984) *Qualitative Data Analysis*, Sage, Beverly Hills.

Oppenheim, A. N. (1992) *Questionnaire Design and Attitude Measurement*, Pinter, London.

Palfrey, C. F., Phillips, C. J. and Thomas, P. (1991) *Economy, Efficiency and Quality of Care*, Social Work Monograph, University of East Anglia.

Palfrey, C. F., Phillips, C., Thomas, P, and Edwards, D. (1992) *Policy Evaluation in the Public Sector: approaches and methods*, Avebury, Aldershot.

Phillipson, C. (1991) 'Elderly people as consumers in the 1990's', *Baseline*, (45) (February), pp. 9–15.

Roghmann, K. J. and Haggerty, R. J. (1972) 'The diary as a research instrument in the study of health and illness behaviour', *Medical Care* 10 (2) pp. 143–63.

St Leger, A. S. *et al.* (1992) *Evaluating Health Services' Effectiveness*, Open University Press, Milton Keynes.

Silverman, D. (1985) *Qualitative Methodology and Sociology*, Gower, Aldershot.

Strauss, A. (1987) *Qualitative Analysis for Social Scientists*, Cambridge University Press.

Sudman, S. and Bradburn, N. (1982) *Asking Questions*, Jossey Bass, New Jersey.

Triandis, H. (1971) *Attitude and Attitude Change*, Wiley, New York.

Whittaker, A., Gardner, S. and Kershaw, J. (1991) *Service Evaluation by People with Learning Difficulties*, The King's Fund Centre, London.

7

Evaluating Equality, Equity and Accessibility

What are equality, equity and accessibility?

Compared with the criteria examined in the previous chapters equality, equity and, to a lesser extent, accessibility are slippery concepts. They have been the subject of much discussion in the context of the reforms in health and social care; but the discussions are not new, and attempts to remove, or at least reduce, inequities and inequalities continue.

So what is meant by 'equality' or 'equity' in health and social care? The concepts are inextricably linked with notions of fairness and justice and attempts to compensate for inequalities may be viewed as part of a broader aim to secure a just settlement or a fair distribution of health and social care provision.

Equality

There are a number of possible avenues to explore in relation to equality. For example we might consider

- equality of opportunity
- equality of access
- equality of utilisation
- equality of outcome.

all of which are difficult to achieve in practice.

For example, an apparent *equality of opportunity* may result in serious inequalities of outcome because some people are better equipped than others to take advantage of the opportunities available; for example, an egalitarian policy of free health care for all cannot prevent Virginia from enjoying a better health status than John, since John's lesser health status may partly be the result of living in a socially deprived area, when Virginia is enjoying the benefits of residing in a relatively affluent area. The opportunities available are thus less equal than they would at first seem.

Equality of access does not necessarily result in *equality of utilisation.* Some people may not perceive that they need the particular service being made available or may wish to purchase health care from a private insurance scheme. Furthermore, *equality of access* is no guarantee of *equality of outcome* since, as Bevan (1990) points out, 'providing equal access to health care may be thought equitable, but if, when patients get there, doctors do different things, is *that* equitable?'

We have suggested elsewhere that a programme was equitable 'if similar outcomes are achieved for people with similar needs' (Palfrey *et al.*, 1990). In this statement there is an element of equality – similar outcomes – but also fairness, in that recipients are people with similar needs. In addition, if *similar services* were provided for people with *differing needs*, this would be regarded as being both inequitable and unjust.

However, this presupposes that the needs of such people have been identified. This in itself is a highly complex area and subject to much debate, yet one which is the primary element in the procurement and provision of care services established under the reforms in health and social care. People's needs have to be assessed and care packages have to be constructed to meet such needs.

1. *Needs*

Needs can be categorised into those which are perceived and those which are not (by the patient, client, carer or advocate). The former relate to those which exist when an 'abnormality' is identified by the patient (or client, etc.) which can be dealt with in one, or a combination, of three ways:

- no action may be taken whatsoever
- use may be made of one of the informal agents involved in health and social care, e.g. self-medication, informal carers
- contact may be made with the health and social services at the initial point of contact (that is, 'expressed need').

However, it may be that the self-perceived needs of the client are not acknowledged as being 'need' by health care and social care professionals but rather as being 'neurosis'. Thus because of this assessment by professionals self-perceived needs would not necessarily be met with service provision.

The other category of needs identified above, namely needs unperceived by the (potential) client, would encompass conditions that are unrecognised by an individual, the family, carers or friends but are potentially discoverable by practitioners and professionals on careful investigation of the total physical, mental and emotional well-being of the individual (Alderson, 1983). The problem is that they only become discoverable when a patient or client actually makes contact with the service providers, who then take on the responsibility of agents acting on behalf of the 'consumer'. Such needs may warrant intervention (when it is thought that prevention, management or specific therapy would be of benefit) but would also include those situations where intervention to meet such needs may prove to be unwanted by the client, e.g. an elderly single person who has been living alone in squalid conditions, surrounded by a large number of pets, for a very long period of time would not, in all probability, welcome a move to a residential or community home.

However, people may have difficulty in identifying or articulating their needs (or indeed wants). This inability to identify needs and wants is limited to levels of knowledge and awareness as to what facilities, services and commodities are available to meet needs and wants. Indeed, one of the primary objectives of advertising is to influence people's perceptions or their wants and needs. Thus suppliers of services are, potentially, in a very advantageous situation when needs have to be assessed, especially when the two functions (assessor and supplier) are contained within the same agency. Other people faced with disabilities may be unable to articulate what their perceptions are and may be forced to rely on advocates.

The importance now attached to meeting people's needs raises the question of whether service provision is client/patient - led or whether the supply of such services is driven by professional, organisational, political and economic interests.

Furthermore, as already indicated, there may not be a coincidence between the views of patients and clients (and their advocates) and those of the professionals regarding needs. The perceptions of GPs, community nurses, social workers and clients/patients may all differ. For example, the relationship between patient and doctor is portrayed in an amusing, but probably reasonably accurate, way by Williams (1990, p. 188):

> At the heart of clinical practice is the doctor/patient relationship. In principle this is a principal–agent relationship in which the patient is principal and the doctor the agent. If a doctor is acting as the perfect agent of his patient, their respective roles would be that the DOCTOR is there to give the PATIENT all the information the PATIENT needs in order that the PATIENT can make a decision, and the DOCTOR should implement that decision once the PATIENT has made it. If that does not sound quite the way it usually is, try reversing the roles of DOCTOR and PATIENT, so that the relationship now gets described as the PATIENT being there to give the DOCTOR all the information the DOCTOR needs in order that the DOCTOR can make a decision, and the PATIENT should then implement that decision once the DOCTOR has made it.

The question as to who should assess the needs to be responded to cannot be answered on empirical grounds alone. The question is ultimately both subjective and political and goes to the very heart of theories of moral justice. What can help in practice is for managers and professionals to be clear about their own particular values and ideas surrounding the notions of justice and equality but also to recognise that other views, in particular those of the client, need to be borne in mind.

2. *The relationship between needs and wants*

It may be that clients' needs do not correspond to their wants – partly because of some needs being identified by someone other than the client and partly because some things that we need might not necessarily be wanted and vice versa. In addition, wants and needs are not independent of the level of supply available, and may be based upon knowledge and awareness of the existence of certain facilities. Such facilities and services have often been provided for elderly people and others requiring care provision by 'agents' on the basis of factors other than their needs or wants. That is not to say that some needs and wants have not been responded to but rather that the supply of health and social services straddles the sets of wants and needs but does not fully meet all of them, as is shown in Figure 7.1.

The proportion of an individual's needs that are actually met by care services is subject to debate, but even if the proportion were approaching 100% for one person this is unlikely to be regarded as equitable or fair if for other people the proportion was much lower. In such a situation inequities and inequalities are possibly being compounded rather than reduced. In addition should those whose own actions create a need for care services (for example, heavy smokers or drug abusers) be treated differently from those who have similar needs through no 'fault' of their own? The notions of 'comparative need' and 'relative need' thus have to be brought into consideration and this is where the professionals have an important role to play, subject to the proviso mentioned above, that they should be prepared to make

Figure 7.1 Wants, needs and supply of services

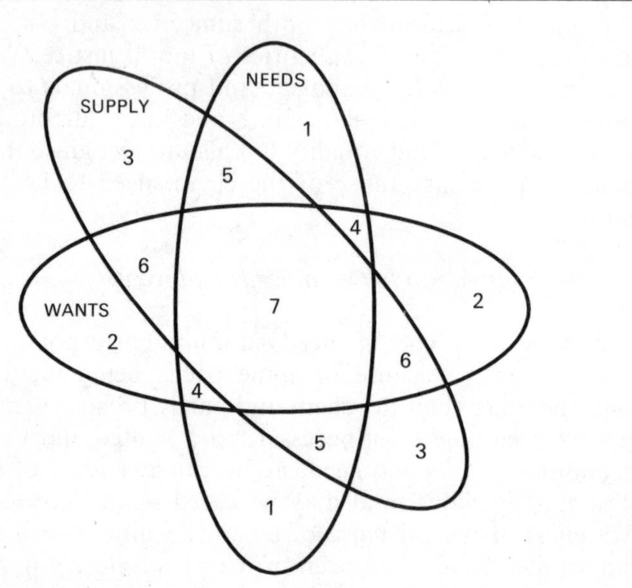

1 Things needed but not wanted nor supplied, e.g. undiagnosed high blood pressure.
2 Things wanted but not needed nor supplied, e.g. demands of neurotic hypochondriacs.
3 Things supplied but not wanted nor needed, e.g. 'trigger happy' surgeons, inappropriate interventions by social workers.
4 Things needed and wanted but not supplied, e.g. waiting lists for treatment.
5 Things needed and supplied but not wanted, e.g. pressures to give up smoking or reduce alcohol consumption.
6 Things wanted and supplied but not needed, e.g. giving neurotic hypochondriacs what they want to make them go away.
7 Things needed and wanted and supplied, e.g. palliative care, caring for elderly dependent people in their own homes.

explicit their own values and ideas of justice and equity and recognise that other views are also important.

Equity

It is possible to categorise equity in terms of *horizontal* and *vertical* equity. The former is concerned with the *equal treatment of equals*, that is, for example, the same treatment for those suffering from the same illness, whilst the latter is concerned with the *unequal treatment of unequals*, for example different packages of care for people with differing needs in relation to dependency and disability. Vertical equity is in practice more difficult to contend with since it requires inequalities to be measured and therefore it is more difficult to cater for in policy terms. As a result of recent policy developments in the field of health and social care, health care agencies and local authority social services departments have been given responsibility to 'purchase' packages of care to cater for the needs of individuals but it is, as yet, unclear how this policy will work in practice in attempting to achieve vertical equity.

The notion of *geographical equity* is one which has been the subject of a number of policy initiatives. For example, resources in the health service were distributed according to a formula designed to reflect to some extent the relative needs of the regions. The formula, established by the Resource Allocation Working Party (RAWP) in the 1970s, attempted to meet the objective of *equal opportunity of access for equal need*.

Another dimension is that of *social equity*, reflected by the findings of *The Health Divide* (Whitehead, 1987) and the Black Report (DHSS, 1980), which demonstrated that those at the bottom of the social scale, in terms of occupational class, employment status and extent of asset holdings, have much higher death rates than those at the top, at every stage of life.

Accessibility

An issue closely related to equality and equity, and already mentioned in passing, is that of *accessibility*. As we have argued elsewhere (Palfrey *et al.*, 1992), if one group has welfare facilities more easily accessible to it than another group, the second group might well feel that the unequal situation is unfair or inequitable. But as with the other criteria examined in this book, the criterion is more complex than it might seem at first sight. The concept has a number of elements.

The first element is *access to goods and services* and to the organisations which provide them: this includes problems of distance, travel times, transport facilities and access for disabled people.

A mechanism used by a number of organisations in recent years – particularly local authorities in relation to their social services and housing functions and health care agencies with their district nursing function – is that of territorial and functional decentralisation. Through locally based 'area offices' or resource centres the public can gain access to social services more easily than in the case of centrally located council offices. The existence of such area offices or resource centres can, therefore, be seen as an attempt to improve accessibility.

Another consideration is the way in which decision-makers distance themselves from the public by appointing 'gatekeepers' (for example, receptionists, switchboard operators and secretaries). Whether or not there are potential obstacles like 'gatekeepers', the availability and approachability of key service providers is an important element of accessibility. Consultant physicians who seem to their clients not to be giving due consideration to their questions and concerns are likely to leave the client feeling that the 'system' is uncaring, unresponsive and inaccessible.

Another aspect of accessibility is the extent to which there are effective mechanisms by which dissatisfied clients may seek *redress of grievances*, for example via courts, inquiries, tribunals, ombudsmen, MPs, councillors, Family Health Service Authorities and Community Health Councils. This array of institutions appears at first sight to be an impressive battery of allies for disgruntled consumers, but the system lacks coherence. The creation of the Patient's Charter does little to improve this situation.

Access to decision-making processes, another piece in the accessibility jigsaw, refers to the extent to which there are genuine opportunities for the public to participate in the decisions about how services are to be provided. The need for public participation in public policy-making and planning has long been recognised (see, for example, the 1969 Skeffington Report), but there is little evidence that any substantial progress has been made in this direction. There is some doubt that the declared aims of the 1989 NHS White Paper (Department of Health, 1989a) and the 1989 Community Care White Paper (Department of Health, 1989b) to give greater 'choice' to the individual contributes much to encouraging, or even allowing, greater public participation in health and social care planning.

As far as *access to information* is concerned, advocates of freedom of information and open government have long argued that British government is too closed in its approach to allowing access to information which affects public policy (see, for example, Wass, 1983; Simey, 1985). An interesting way to look at this problem is to ask 'whose information is it ?' We do not mean by this who has the legal right to the information in question, but who *ought* to have such a legal right.

In each of the above cases there are questions of the *right* of access, the *ease* of access, and the *cost* of access. For a hospital patient's family to be told that they are allowed to visit 'at any time' is little consolation if the hospital is thirty miles from where they (and the patient) live, especially if they have a low income and no car.

Why are equality, equity and accessibility important?

It is generally accepted that these criteria are important social and political goals, which have been at the very heart of discussions relating to health and social care. However, despite differing approaches to reducing inequalities, depending upon the prevailing political climate, evidence of inequities, inequalities and problems of accessibility abound at all levels, within and across societies.

The pattern of inequalities in health in the 1970s was thoroughly documented by the Black Report (DHSS, 1980) while *The Health Divide* (Whitehead, 1987) provided evidence to demonstrate that 'serious social inequalities in health have persisted into the 1980s'. These reports argued that the poor were affected to a greater extent than the rich by the killer diseases and higher rates of chronic sickness were found amongst the lower occupational groups as well as their children tending to have lower birthweight and shorter stature. In addition, the unemployed and their families have considerably worse physical and mental health than those in work and areas of the country with relatively high levels of unemployment have worse health records than areas with low levels of unemployment.

The debate surrounding unemployment, ill-health and mortality has attracted considerable interest and discussion concerning the strength of the relationship amongst these variables. Is it the case that unemployment causes an increase in morbidity and mortality or is it the opposite, that poor health and illness are a cause of unemployment? (For further reading in this area see for example Brenner, 1979; Stern, 1983.)

Regional disparities in health are also the subject of debate. *The Health Divide* (Whitehead 1987) pointed out that death rates in various parts of the country confirmed 'the long established North/South gradient'. However, it has been argued that the 'focus of most previous research has been on male deaths between 25 and 64. This is a small, selected group of the population in which most of the deaths occur in the 45–64 age group. Focusing on this group ignores the mortality experience of younger and older age groups, where the vast majority of deaths occur; and that shows a narrowing, and even in some cases elimination, of the regional health divide' (Ilsley *et al.*, 1991).

In addition, *The Health Divide* (Whitehead, 1987) pointed to studies which provided evidence of great inequalities between adjacent communities in the same region, with affluent communities enjoying relatively good health whilst the areas suffering from social and material deprivation experience very poor health. One of the most striking conclusions of the report was that such health inequalities have been widening in recent decades (even allowing for the difficulties in measuring health trends over time). However, Ilsley and Le Grand (1987) concluded that those diseases which contributed most to mortality among the poor (infectious and respiratory diseases) declined in importance to such an extent during this period that there may have been a reduction in the health inequality between rich and poor. This debate has continued with Townsend (1990) re-affirming the principal policy recommendation of the Black Report 'that the most beneficial development for the health of the population is a massive assault on material deprivation – through improvement of low incomes and the incomes in particular of families with children, retirement pensioners and people with disabilities, and improvement of the material conditions of the home, the workplace and the environment'.

Very closely linked to inequalities in health are the other areas where inequalities exist. For example, the close correlation between housing conditions and health is well documented (see, for example, Byrne, 1986; Whitehead, 1987; Smith, 1989) and it is not surprising to discover that those people living in poor quality housing experience much worse health than those living in better quality housing.

How to assess equality, equity and accessibility?

The Black Report (DHSS, 1980) concentrated on the use of mortality rates amongst social groups to arrive at a measure of health inequality.

However, Ilsley (1986) questioned the validity of such an approach because it failed to consider changes in the relative size of the groups over time. He demonstrated that there was a dramatic reduction in inequality between the top and bottom social classes if the absolute number of deaths in each group was compared over time.

Other studies have attempted to combine several indicators of social and material deprivation into *composite indices of deprivation*, thereby allowing areas to be ranked according to the degree of disadvantage or affluence according to their particular score.

For example, *Jarman's Underprivileged Area Score* (Jarman, 1983, 1984) is based on a number of social variables selected on the basis of a survey of GPs' work-load patterns:

- percentage of children aged under 5
- percentage of unemployed
- poor housing
- percentage of ethnic minorities
- percentage of single-parent households
- percentage of elderly living alone
- overcrowding factor
- percentage of lower social classes
- percentage of highly mobile people
- percentage of non-married family groups.

Another example is that of the *Material Deprivation Score* (Townsend *et al.*, 1988). Here the index is constructed on the basis of:

- percentage of households with fewer rooms than persons
- percentage of households lacking a car
- percentage of economically active persons seeking work (or temporarily sick)
- percentage of homes that are not owner occupied.

Obviously there are a number of limitations attached to indices such as those above and others. For example, some combine direct indicators of deprivation, such as unemployment and households lacking basic amenities, with indirect measures which indicate the number of people at risk of deprivation, such as the proportion of elderly people or ethnic minorities in an area. However, in these groups not all of the people are deprived and therefore the index does not provide a true reflection of the actual situation. Furthermore, as Thunhurst (1985) suggests, the incorporation of highly skewed variables, such as ethnic minority households and one-parent families, can lead to misleading results.

The Jarman index, for example, results in a large proportion of the most deprived health districts being in London, with none in the North of England. A study comparing the Jarman and Townsend methods discovered that if the Townsend score was used instead of the Jarman index the Northern and Mersey region would gain over 50% of their allocation of resources whereas East Anglia, Oxford and South West Thames would lose more than 30% of theirs, (Hutchinson *et al.*, 1989). This has serious policy implications, since the Jarman index is utilised to determine which GPs are entitled to receive payments for practising in 'underprivileged areas'. The problems associated with such scores have meant that the Welsh Office, for example, has incorporated other variables in the formula designed to identify areas of deprivation for purposes of GP remuneration in Wales. For a more detailed discussion of these measures see, for example, Carr-Hill (1990); O'Donnell and Propper (1989); Ilsley and Le Grand (1987); Townsend (1990); and Whitehead (1987).

Situations obviously arise where 'competing organisations' would argue in favour of 'instruments' which resulted in the best outcome for themselves. One therefore needs to be sceptical when advocates are arguing for their preferred procedure for assessing inequalities.

Case studies

In order to highlight some of the issues and complexities discussed two case studies are used.

Example 1: home care services

A local authority social service department is about to reorganise its home care services. The authority is divided into five social services areas, with areas A, D and E each having its own home care organiser whilst areas B and C have one home care organiser between them. Areas B and C are primarily rural with much lower population densities than areas A, D and E but with a greater proportion of elderly in the 75+ age bracket and a greater proportion of single occupancy of houses. However, there are fewer home care assistants and a much lower average number of home care hours per client in the rural areas.

The department has tried to remedy the problem but has experienced difficulties in recruiting home care assistants from within areas B and C and the implications for the travelling expenses budget has precluded the deployment of home care assistants from areas A, D and E.

If you were responsible for the reorganisation of home care services suggest some potential remedies to reduce the inequities and inequalities which exist under the current system.

There may be a number of possible remedies:

1 The authority may have to sacrifice some efficiency in order to ensure that service provision is the same in all areas by, for example, employing an additional home care organiser for areas B and C; employing home care assistants for more hours in areas B and C thus equalising the average number of hours per client; offering additional incentives to counter the recruitment problems; and increasing the travelling allowance budget (reductions elsewhere) to compensate for the 'rural effect'.
2 There may have to be a diminution of services in areas A, D and E to equalise service provision within the authority, that is a possible loss of effectiveness in order to achieve equality and equity.
3 A different type of service provision might have to be considered in areas B and C with more flexible use of

local staff and some degree of input from staff from areas A, D and E.

4 The recruitment problems in rural areas could be addressed by, for example, asking neighbours of potential service users if they would provide help at certain times of the day for some remuneration; employing people for shorter durations so as not to affect benefit payments.

Example 2: GP practice accommodation

A GP practice has to find new accommodation because the current practice is located in a converted house which is part of the estate of the recently deceased senior partner.

A large new private housing estate has land allocated for a new health centre and, because demographic trends do not warrant the establishment of another practice, the FHSA has approved plans for the practice to move to this purpose-built accommodation. The estate has a range of houses from one-bedroom starter homes to large executive-type houses, which are increasing in proportion because they are still relatively attractive despite the depressed housing market.

The community where the practice has been located for many years is an area with an ageing population living in private housing, the vast majority of the stock being at least thirty years old. Nearby is an area consisting of a mixture of council houses, housing association property and ex-council houses, where the levels of unemployment are relatively high, the incidence of crime and vandalism is increasing and there are a few community homes for patients discharged from a mental hospital scheduled for closure.

What are the implications for accessibility to the new practice and what are the likely consequences for health inequalities between groups in the locality? In what ways can the FHSA offset these problems?

The obvious inference is that accessibility for the community where the practice has been located is considerably reduced. Given the description of the communities it is likely that the health inequalities between the different groups will be increased, unless arrangements can be made to offset the consequences of the relocation. However, the information does not contain any details of transport and road links between the current location and the new accommodation. The FHSA could seek to ensure that frequent, regular public transport is provided between the two locations, or even provide their own transport if no other appropriate public transport is available, so as to minimise the obvious difficulties caused by the relocation.

The FHSA could also negotiate with the district health authority over the possibility of establishing a *branch surgery* in one of the community homes, which would enable those for whom the new journey to the GP practice was excessively burdensome to attend at a more convenient location.

There may be an alternative view that the purpose-built accommodation will result in a more efficient service being provided and thus the reduction in accessibility and consequential increase in inequalities can be satisfactorily offset by the increase in efficiency.

Difficulties in evaluating equality, equity and accessibility

There is an obvious problem in seeking to evaluate a programme against criteria, the precise definitions of which are far from clear. Further, because the lack of widely recognised and accepted measures makes it difficult to assess the inequalities and inequities prior to and after the programme has been implemented, serious problems are likely to arise in attempting to measure and evaluate change.

As was seen in the above examples, additional problems arise because of the interrelationships (sometimes referred to as the 'trade-off') between equity and some of the other criteria involved in the evaluation process. In attempting to reduce inequalities through public policy measures there may well be consequences for other objectives of the policy (for example, effectiveness and efficiency). Le Grand (1990) cites the case of a health care programme designed to highlight the dangers of smoking, which would increase the average life expectancy of all groups in the population thereby promoting efficiency, but which would promote a greater increase in life expectancy for the better-off, because they may, for a number of reasons, be more responsive to the message, consequently increasing inequality. Similarly, programmes designed to improve accessibility to services, such as community based hospitals, may not prove to be as efficient as the concentration of facilities in larger district hospitals.

Summary and checklist

At the crudest level it should be possible to determine what the potential beneficiaries of a programme have prior to its implementation and who gets what as a result of the programme. However, to progress beyond such a crude approach involves further discussion as to what measures ought to be adopted. Ultimately, one has to decide upon a measure, or a combination of measures, and utilise them. Despite the limitations of the measure(s) some attempt should be made to consider the impact of the programme in reducing (or widening) inequalities and inequities between groups and/or regions within the area, county or country.

The following checklist adapted from Whitehead (1991) may provide a starting point.

1 Given that many inequalities exist as a result of poor living and working conditions, does the programme seek to improve such conditions?
2 Does the programme aim to assist people to adopt healthier life-styles, and provide support mechanisms to enable them to maintain those changes against negative social pressures?

3 Has the programme been designed and provided as a result of assessments of what people actually need and require rather than what the provider organisations wish to provide?
4 Since authorities need to be conscious of the health and social consequences of public policies generally, is the underlying framework that of a holistic model of health and social care? For example, is enough account taken of the impact of health upon unemployment and vice versa, or the social and health implications of location of industry?
5 Has the marketing of the programme been carefully thought through to ensure that access and utilisation are not distributed inequitably?
6 Does the policy include the monitoring of the distribution of outcomes so as to ensure that no one group (social, geographic, etc.) receives an unfair share and other groups do not benefit at all, especially within the context of finite resources?
7 What are the effects of the policy or service on the *distribution* of costs and benefits – for example, who pays and who gains?
8 To what extent have individuals' perceptions of their needs and wants been taken into consideration?

References

Alderson, M. (1983) *An Introduction to Epidemiology*, Macmillan, Basingstoke.

Bevan, G. (1990) 'Equity and variability in modern health care', in Andersen, T. F. and Mooney, G., *The Challenges of Medical Practice Variations*, Macmillan, Basingstoke.

Brenner, M. H. (1979) 'Mortality and the National Economy: a review, and the experience of England and Wales 1936–1976', *The Lancet*, 2(8142) pp. 568–73.

Byrne, D. S. *et al.* (1986) *Housing and Health: the relationship between housing conditions and the health of council tenants*, Gower, Aldershot.

Carr-Hill, R. (1990) 'The measurement of inequities in health: lessons from the British experience', *Social Science and Medicine*, 31 (3), pp. 393–404.

Culyer, A. J. and Wagstaff, A. (1992) *Need, Equity and Equality in Health and Health Care*, Centre for Health Economics Discussion Paper 95, University of York.

Department of Health (1989a) *Working for Patients*, HMSO, London.

Department of Health (1989b) *Caring for People*, Cmnd. 555. HMSO, London.

Department of Health and Social Security (1980) *Inequalities in Health*, Report of a research working group chaired by Sir Douglas Black, DHSS, London.

Hutchinson, A. *et al.* (1989) 'Comparison of two scores for allocating resources to doctors in deprived areas', *British Medical Journal*, 299, (6708), pp. 1142–44.

Ilsley, R. (1986) 'Occupational class, selection and the production of inequalities in health', *Quarterly Journal of Social Affairs*, 2, (2), pp. 151–65.

Ilsley, R. *et al.* (1991) *Regional Inequalities in Mortality*, Welfare State Programme, *Discussion Paper*, 57, London School of Economics and Political Science, London.

Ilsley, R. and Le Grand, J. (1987) 'The measurement of inequality in health', in Williams, A. (ed.) *Health and Economics*, Macmillan, London.

Jarman, B. (1984) 'Under-privileged areas: validation and distribution', *British Medical Journal*, 289, pp. 1587–92.

Jarman, B. (1983) 'Identification of underprivileged areas', *British Medical Journal*, 286, pp. 1705–9.

Le Grand, J. (1990) 'Equity versus efficiency: the elusive trade-off', *Ethics*, 100 (April), pp. 554–68.

O'Donnell, O. and Propper, C. (1989) *Equity and the Distribution of National Health Service Resources*, Welfare State Programme, *Discussion Paper* 45, London School of Economics and Political Science, London.

Palfrey, C. F. *et al.* (1990) 'Jargon into practice', *Community Care*, 9 (November), pp. 15–16.

Palfrey, C., Phillips, C., Thomas, P. and Edwards, D. (1992) *Policy Evaluation in the Public Sector: approaches and methods*, Avebury, Aldershot.

Simey, M. (1985) *Government by Consent*, Bedford Square Press, London.

Skeffington Report (1969) *People and Planning: Report of the Committee on Public Participation in Planning*, HMSO, London.

Smith, S. J. (1989) *Housing and Health: a review and research agenda*, Centre for Housing Research, *Discussion Paper* 27, Glasgow.

Stern, J. (1983) 'The relationship between unemployment, morbidity and mortality in Britain', *Population Studies*, 37, pp. 61–74.

Thunhurst, C. (1985) 'The analysis of small area statistics and planning for health', *The Statistician*, 34, pp. 93–106.

Townsend, P. (1990) 'Widening inequalities of health in Britain: a rejoinder to Rudolph Klein', *International Journal of Health Services*, 20 (3), pp. 363–72.

Townsend, P. *et al.* (1988) *Health and Deprivation: inequality and the North*, Croom Helm, London.

Wass, D. (1983) *Government and the Governed*, BBC Reith Lectures, RKP, London.

Whitehead, M. (1991) 'The concepts and principles of equity and health', *Health Promotion International*, 6 (3), pp. 217–28.

Whitehead, M. (1987) *The Health Divide*, Health Education Council, London.

Williams, A. (1990) 'Ethics, clinical freedom and the doctors' role', in Culyer, A. J. *et al.*, *Competition in Health Care: Reforming the NHS*, Macmillan, Basingstoke.

8

Summing Up

Traditionally, assessment of the relative success or failure of a particular policy or programme in health and social care has tended to be made largely on the basis of impressionistic or anecdotal evidence with the evidence provided by the more *powerful* groups carrying the greatest weight.

However, more recently there has been a demand for more systematic assessment of programmes and policies, with the purpose of determining the extent to which aims and objectives are achieved and the impact programmes have on specific groups and on society as a whole.

This book has sought to demonstrate that in undertaking such evaluations, there is no single 'best' approach to adopt and that there is no one criterion against which one should judge a policy or programme. Rather the emphasis has been on the range of designs that may be utilised, the differing types and sources of data that can be used and the variety of criteria which need to be considered, even if, at the end of the day, one may have to be *traded-off* against another. The advantages of this pluralistic approach have been summarised by Smith and Cantley (1985), who argue that:

- it provides a complicated but realistic answer to the question of whether a service is successful or not
- it has the potential to explain why 'failures' in service provision occur. The evaluation looks at process as well as outcome
- this explanation opens the way for change

- pluralistic evaluation readily details some of the costs of success, e.g. the unanticipated consequences of policies
- the approach can also facilitate the implementation of research results because it is less likely that stakeholders will argue that their interests have not been taken into account
- it stands some chance of remaining 'independent' and 'neutral' by taking sympathetic account of as many perspectives as possible.

The book has also sought to show that *all* who are committed to improving service provision can be involved, including customers and consumers. Managers and professionals operating in an era of *user involvement, needs - led provision* and *consumerism* have very little choice but to get involved in assessing what they do, how they do it, why they do it, what is achieved, who is affected and so on.

It is hoped that the ideas suggested in this book will be taken up by all those who strive for effective, efficient, accessible and equitable health and social care services where the consumer voice is not only heard, but recognised as an important factor to be considered in decisions relating to the delivery of services.

Reference

Smith, G. and Cantley, C. (1985) *Assessing Health Care: A study in organisational evaluation*, Open University Press, Milton Keynes.

Index